For Zsa Zsa always,

To our son, Jordan, and our daughter, Sydney;

in hopes that their world will be better than ours

Contents

Foreword

There is a sharp edge of contemporeneity to everything that
Daniel Smith-Christopher writes. As a shrewd reader of texts,
he shows how and why it is that the texts rush among us evoca-
tively, raising questions for us and issuing commands to us. In
this discussion the controlling metaphor is "coyotes" (*polleros*),
the current term for those who help immigrants evade the
authorities in order to cross the border into the United States.
Smith-Christopher ponders the way in which constructed borders of all kinds create division, hostility, and conflict. But his
accent point concerns the work of "crossing the borders" with
passion, refusing to honor or take serious artificial borders, crossing them for the sake of freedom, justice, and well-being. His
inventory of ancient "border crossers," in addition to Jonah and
Jesus named in the title, includes Second Isaiah who refused the
old imperial arrangements. Each of the "crossers" dared to violate borders in order to create new human possibility. The bite of
this splendid exposition is the current gospel summons to cross
borders, to eschew old divisions, and thereby make healing possible. The author uses impressive learning as an accomplished
critic to give access to the rich, subversive claims of the text. The
book authorizes new thinking about faith and new action in obedience. This is an important read combining erudition and passion of the most immediate kind.

Walter Brueggemann
Columbia Theological Seminary

Acknowledgments

The work that follows resulted from interesting conversations between Dr. John Kutsko of Abingdon Press and me. John asked if I would consider trying to write an "accessible, even popular level" book dealing with the reading the Bible and peacemaking. *Jonah, Jesus, and Other Good Coyotes* is the result of those conversations, and I have tried to live up to John's challenge in the work that follows. This book is, therefore, written to be less an academic argument than a series of suggestions for study and thought. Because of the strict instructions to keep footnotes to an absolute minimum, I want to acknowledge that many of my colleagues whose work I have read with great appreciation will recognize some of their influence in what follows, and I want to thank them for their work. I would like to especially mention, however, my appreciation for the work of Bob Ekblad, whose work I discuss in the opening chapter.

I want to express my sincere appreciation to Abingdon Press for this invitation to write, and to everyone there who helped to bring my sometimes difficult prose into readable form. Any failures that readers will find in what follows are entirely my own. I want to also thank my friend, Rev. Don Tamihere of Gisborne, New Zealand, who read over the manuscript. Finally, I want to express my appreciation for the continued encouragement from Walter Brueggemann, whose work many of us aspire to emulate in both erudition and clarity.

Introduction

An Epistle from California

All Biblical Studies come from a "place." What this means is that all readings and interpretations are influenced by the experience, background, and context of the reader of the Bible. In the case of the writer of this book, the "place" from which I am reading the Bible and writing about the Bible has had a major impact on how I think about the Bible. Why is this important? I live in Southern California, and an ever-present reality for all of us in this location is the United States/Mexico border. This border, however, is more than merely a national boundary. This particular border has become a symbol, virtually a shrine. As a Christian, I am deeply worried about the attitudes toward, and events that take place at this "shrine." There is a kind of nearly religious "worship" that goes on there.

This particular border has become a shrine to false national pride, a shrine to greed (fed by the availability of desperate and hungry workers), and a shrine to American refusal to face our own racism and our responsibility for the suffering of fellow human beings because—once again—those fellow humans are darker skinned and live across a border that we ourselves largely created. In short, whenever a thing, a creation, becomes so important that people suffer over it, it has become an idol. This border has become an idol.

Throughout this book, I will be talking about all kinds of borders that separate humans from each other—borders that protect interests and borders that inspire conflict. I know very well, however, that my approach to reading the Bible as a call to "cross human borders" is deeply connected to my daily awareness of the idol that exists only a few hours south of where I am writing these words. All Christians, however, know what I am talking about when I speak of false borders and false separations that humans create.

BIBLICAL PEACEMAKING MEANS "RUNNING BORDERS"

In the modern world, "borders" tend to cultivate division and conflict. Sometimes the very act of creating borders, or shifting borders, creates conflict. Those who want to help people get along better with each other in this world often speak of borders negatively, pointing to the unhappy reality that borders separate us from one another. It is also true that virtually all social, political, and international borders exist only in the minds of people and most often, in the minds of the powerful.

Borders can sometimes be a useful fiction, helpfully demarcating differences between peoples, cultures, faiths, and other groups. Borders may, for example, indicate places considered sacred or special to particular peoples and cultures. In these cases, the borders are not to keep people out, but to educate people of the importance of the place and to ask for respect. Borders may be friendly requests to understand differences between traditions. These differences are good things; they result from the variety, diversity, and possibilities that enrich human life. At their best, borders highlight the friendly distinctions between groups, reminding us to recognize and honor those differences.

However, borders have a nasty habit of becoming excuses for conflict, bigotry, and ultimately, war. When this happens, Christians must remember the biblical lesson that making peace between groups of people often requires that *somebody* must be willing to intentionally and peacefully cross the borders that separate potentially hostile groups so that conversations can begin, trust be restored, and hope be revived for peace. In this book, I argue that the Bible teaches Christians that we are called to be this "somebody." We are called to violate borders in the name of Jesus Christ.

I do not speak of violent border running. Violating borders, as in military assaults or colonial attacks on indigenous peoples, is partially a refusal to respect differences, and this legacy is an unacceptable violation of cultural "borders." This is not the kind of positive "border running" that I am advocating for Christians, especially in North America, Australia, and New Zealand. This much is clear. How do we know when borders become an idol that we should stop worshiping? I have some suggestions.

READING THE "WARNING SIGNS"

In an ironic sense, borders become warning signs when borders actually **display** warning signs. Dangerous developments are evident when people talk about the goodness of everyone on "our" side of the border, and the evil of everyone on the "other" side. Being a part of a group is not inherently bad, of course, nor is believing in the importance of the traditions of your group, culture, or faith. But in the modern world too many otherwise innocent borders have threatened to become dangerous grounds for bigotry, greed, and open hostility. Patriotism, for example, has tended in recent years to become a corrupted and self-righteous arrogance toward people outside "our" borders. I argue in this book that it is time for the people of God, especially the followers of Jesus, to become suspicious of all talk about "protecting our borders" when it is spoken with violent hatred of "the others"—namely, those on the other side of the lines we have invented in our minds or lines we have imposed on others.

The fact is, the most dangerous borders that Western Christians should be willing to violate were made by our own national or economic pride. Running borders is, therefore, usually going to be—at the same time we are running them—an act of confession that we ourselves once participated in violently creating the border we cross. After all, who are we usually seeking to meet by our acts of biblical "border running"? Often it is the very people our nations once tried to shut out, reject, or despise. Biblical border running means seeking to be reconciled to the "others."

Many modern social commentators now use the generic phrase "the other" to refer to the unfortunate tendency of human groups to seek a more positive image of themselves by contrasting it with negative images of people in other groups, or simply, "the other." If we feel bad about "our" group, we can always point to an "other" group and try to make that group look worse. The "other" can be any kind of group—a nation with whom we are preparing to go to war, a racial group within our nation, a religious group within our nation (notice how easily the borders can change from national borders to local borders to social borders or religious borders). In virtually every case of creating borders, the differences between people have the potential to enflame violence. Instead of enjoying the differences between groups and the joyful discovery of new ideas, new traditions, and new experiences that can come from those differences, it seems that some people need to condemn others to feel better about themselves. If this human tendency gets mixed up with business interests—in other words, if somebody is making money from negative attitudes about "the other"—then there is serious potential for people to get hurt. For example, mix together oil money, defense contractors, political power, and religious differences, stir in bigoted concerns about "our borders," and you have the dangerous and explosive mix that characterizes so much of life at the dawn of the third millennium.

Consider, for example, how Samuel Huntington's discussion of the "Clash of Civilizations"[1] has led a number of American political and social leaders to believe there is an inevitable conflict between "cultures," especially the "West" versus the Islamic world. Many commentators have responded to Huntington's analysis by pointing out that such talk amounts to self-fulfilling prophecy when it falls on the ears of those unable or unwilling to reach out and cross borders in the name of peace and understanding.[2] They remind us that creatively violating borders sometimes begins when we ask why the borders in question became so important in the first place.

When some minority groups have suffered persecution or violence, they understandably react by developing a strong internal sense of the goodness of their group identity, and this often goes along with disparaging attitudes toward those who harmed them. This kind of border—and the hurt and anger that produced it—can frighten the dominant group on the "other side," whose response is usually to throw up borders of their own. But the more biblical response would be to offer (typically long overdue) apologies to any group in pain with assurances that the abuses should not continue. Ignoring this hurt and anger (or worse, denying the abuses that produced them in the first place) leads only to an increased cycle of suspicion, distrust, and hatred. In fact, our expressed willingness to listen will usually result in our being invited to cross such defensive borders.

Usually, however, this edging closer to the borders in order to listen is cut short because we do not want to listen to anger or admit that injustices have occurred, and a basic human response is to try to return to feeling good about "my border" by avoiding or even dehumanizing "them" or denying "their" history. So, the borders become locations of trouble; the shouting continues; the anger builds.

How do we get back to joyful coexistence? How do we return to learning from each other and enjoying our differences without feeling threatened? Someone must demonstrate the value of violating those borders that have become cruel separations between people who should coexist. As I said earlier, Christians are that "someone."

WAR AND BORDERS

War, of course, is an ultimate expression of these resentments across borders. The horrendous sacrifices necessary for warfare require huge efforts to create bad feelings about potential enemies. History teaches us that many political and religious leaders often enhance their power, wealth, and authority by feeding this mistrust of others, advocating stronger "borders," and especially by shouting that "our borders are in danger." One particularly effective way to strengthen power is to dehumanize the "other," claiming that we can never trust "those people," that they want to destroy our way of life, or that they are not civilized like us.

Sometimes those who are hungry for power use the language of infection to dehumanize groups of people *within* the dominant group's own imagined borders. This kind of language suggests that the "health of the body" is at stake, requiring the removal of the infection. Left unchecked, those who denounce the infection will use it to justify genocidal violence, like the destruction of Muslim Bosnians, Tutsi Rwandans, Jewish Germans, Turkish Armenians, Native Americans, or any of a hundred other similar groups.[3]

Is the creation and maintenance of these kinds of human borders and conflicts really so important for us to study as Christians? I would invite American Christians to consider the fact that in virtually every conflict the United States has engaged in, the preparations for war have involved massive expenditures by our government (and often private business interests) to convince the general population that the conflict is necessary and that the enemy is worthy only of being destroyed.[4] I believe, however, that Christians have deeply biblical reasons for being suspicious of any attempt to get us to accept the dehumanizing of any other human being or human group. After all, the book of Revelation likewise points to a time when Christians were part of a suspect and persecuted minority. All of us who claim the biblical story as our own, then, should remember that we were once the "other." We should always question the language of hate and separation, of building up borders.

Being a part of a tradition—a Christian church, a mosque, a synagogue, a movement, a cultural group—can be deeply rewarding, fulfilling, and meaningful. But what do we do when group loyalties (the innocent "borders" of membership and participation) turn into borders of separation and hatred? The Bible suggests that, in these circumstances, some unusual people need to be willing to run borders in the name of peace. Again, the Bible teaches that those unusual people are Christians. We are those people.

A BIBLICAL RESPONSE: "GOOD COYOTES" WHO RUN BORDERS

Somebody has to have the courage to "cross the border," be willing to listen, and overcome the desire to make the borders tighter and more secure whenever we feel criticized. In his book *Reading the Bible with the Damned*, Pastor Bob Ekblad describes what he has learned by working with immigrant and migrant workers in the state of Washington. One image that he discussed struck me deeply as I was preparing this book and already thinking about the image of "border running." He notes the negative perception of border runners between the United States and Mexico, especially the individuals known as *polleros,* or "coyotes," who help people from Central and South America cross the Mexico/United States border in search of work. The general assumption is that these professional "coyotes" are invariably evil people. Television, film, and newspapers generally portray "coyotes" as unscrupulous men and women who always exploit the poverty of the Latin Americans who want to get work in the United States. And this is often true—there are hundreds of horror stories of "bad coyotes" mistreating poor immigrants who only want to find a better life.

What surprised Pastor Ekblad, however, was the fact that many immigrants described experiences with "good coyotes." These are people who use the money they are paid to make sure that the people crossing the borders are fed, taken care of, and have safe passage. I found a story about "coyotes" printed in *USA Today* (Dec. 1, 2003), in which the writer interviewed many immigrants and came to realize that "Migrants don't see them as the bad guy in the movie . . . . Many call them heroes because they got them and their families across the border. If you ask them, they will say, 'Thanks to the *pollero,* I'm in the United States.

Thanks to the *pollero*, my mother, my children, my grandfather are in the United States.'" So, is there such a thing as a "good" coyote?

Pastor Ekblad then introduced a startling idea. He compared Jesus to a "good coyote" because Jesus invites us to cross borders—often violating, for the sake of the gospel, the loyalties we humans have built to separate us from one another. As I began to write this book I was already thinking about the concept of violating borders, and in a conversation Dr. Ekblad graciously encouraged me to use his idea. Perhaps it isn't so unusual that I found the idea of Jesus as a "good coyote" such a wonderful and provocative image. I am, after all, the product of a Quaker family.

It is arguably the case that Quakers have been fulfilling the role of the "good coyote" throughout American history. In the 1980s, many Quakers participated in the sanctuary movement along the United States/Mexico border. They intentionally violated U.S. border laws in order to provide asylum for Latin Americans escaping torture in countries that had ties to the United States. Because of these official American ties to the right-wing governments in the countries from which these refugees came, the Reagan administration refused to classify these people as refugees and would not allow them into the country legally. Jim Corbett, the Quaker organizer who was a leader of this movement, is a model good coyote. Step back further into history and you will find many more Quaker coyotes smuggling slaves northwards in the Underground Railroad.

There is a great Willie Nelson song that says, "My heroes have always been cowboys...." As I thought about it, I realized that my heroes have always been good coyotes. Harriet Tubman—the famous "Black Moses" who led over three hundred slaves to the North and freedom in nineteenth-century America—was a famous "good coyote." John Howard Griffin, a devoted layman in the Catholic church, colored his skin black in 1959 in order to travel in the segregated South. After some months experiencing just a little bit of what it meant to be black in the South under repressive laws and traditions, he wrote *Black Like Me*, a work often criticized but still taught in thousands of classrooms as a way to understand some of the realities of racism in the United States. I think of Uri Avnery, the Israeli activist who persisted in meeting with Yasser Arafat even when it was illegal to meet with the "enemy," or Issam Sartawi, the Palestinian doctor who gave up organized military resistance to Israel in order to pursue peaceful negotiations and died at the hands of hardliners among his own people because of his willingness to continue to meet with Israelis to discuss peace. I think of Taner Akçam, the Turkish historian who openly and compassionately writes of the truth of the Armenian genocides in the early twentieth century, infuriating some other Turks who still deny that it ever took place. I think at the same time of Dr. Ronald G. Suny, the Armenian historian who has accepted invitations, even in Turkey itself, to lecture on the genocide, and who regularly engages in dialogue with any Turks willing to talk. I think of Mahmoud Taha, the "African Gandhi," a Muslim teacher who defended equal rights for all Sudanese women and also for Christians in southern Sudan. I think of those brave critics of the historic Crusades, like Isaac de l'Etoile, who spoke out against the medieval Christian hatred that fed those horrible wars against Islam and referred to the recently founded medieval military orders as "monstrosities." And I think of John Woolman, the nineteenth-century American Quaker who refused to wear dyed cloth because it was produced by slaves. I have been deeply moved by the stories I have heard from Lawrence Hart, one of the council chiefs of the southern Cheyenne. These stories are about the Cheyenne traditional peace chief whose duty (accepted by an oath to the tribe) was to physically run and stand between his own people's warriors and enemy lines in order to try and stop all conflicts. As I write this, our own Cardinal Roger Mahony of the Roman Catholic Archdiocese of Los Angeles has once again risked ridicule and anger by calling for compassion for aliens and immigrants in California and refusing to go along with proposed laws that would require abusive practices toward illegal aliens. My heroes have always been coyotes.[5]

So, I am sympathetic to the need to doubt, and even to violate, borders at times in the name of peace and justice. Recently, however, I have begun to realize that "holy border running" is a deeply scriptural concept, rooted especially in the Old Testament. I want to argue, therefore, that biblical peacemaking begins with being willing to run borders.

The Old Testament roots of biblical peacemaking do not rest in a moral or theological criticism of violence. That would be looking for a modern-style argument in an ancient text, which is precisely what I was looking for as a student of the Bible for many years. It has taken me a long time to come to my belief that the Old Testament speaks of peacemaking in very unique ways, and I simply did not recognize it. It is true that there are few voices in the Old Testament that openly criticize violence and war, and many voices that seem to openly advocate violence and war. But the peace voices are there. In fact, the Old Testament concept of peacemaking centers around border crossing. Old Testament peacemaking begins with those who risk challenging old loyalties and borders and reach out to the "others." It starts with people who begin to question the official explanations, the official bias, the official versions, and then suggest alternative, border-violating ways of thinking. It was only when I started to listen that I began to hear them: Hebrew coyotes!

When the Old Testament refers to the "other," it generally uses the term *the nations*. More to the point, it refers to them negatively. The clear message of many texts in the Old Testament is: "The nations are bad; we are good." Borders are well maintained. But the Bible also gives a voice to a courageous minority, beginning in the Old Testament and continuing in the New Testament. This is the voice of the border runners, the good coyotes who challenge their people's anger and violence toward those on the other side of the border by speaking well of, and even acting on the hope for a more peaceful relationship with the "others."

To summarize the argument of this book, I believe that the Old Testament good coyotes planted the seeds for the rise of a later radical group of Hebrew border runners who came to be called

Christians. I will try in this book to suggest ways in which we can hear them again.

I hope, however, that readers will do more than simply hear the voices of biblical coyotes. The result of this study will be, I hope, a new way of thinking about peacemaking from a biblical perspective. I also hope that it will lead to some Christians deciding to flagrantly violate human borders between groups in the name of peace and justice. I hope it will lead to local Christians deciding to risk meeting with "others" in their towns and cities, maybe in other countries and nations.

Biblical history can teach us that Christian churches should become places where people of all backgrounds meet to talk (perhaps even to argue, if necessary) about achieving a way to work together, coexisting and building our society together with all kinds of people of all sorts of backgrounds. I hope that reading this book might lead some Christians to ask serious questions about what we are told to believe about "those people"—the others. When it comes to listening to the powerful, who often try to tell us who to hate, the Bible teaches Christians to become holy skeptics. If anyone can, perhaps we can find our own ways to meet those "others" and discover who they really are. I also hope that reading the Bible will lead many Christians to radically rethink their ideas about who our enemies really are—whether it be the enemies we are fighting now, or the enemies we are being told to be careful about, or the enemies we are told are among us.

I dream of church basements, university halls, or public cafes, where coffee will be poured, and sweets offered across the tables where strangers have decided to meet. Such meetings will probably be somewhat tentative at first—perhaps even reluctant at first—as we learn to sit down together and violate the borders between us. I hope some Christians will learn to refuse to believe anyone or anything that tells them that respect for their own "borders" (their traditions, their communities) can only be accomplished by hating others. I hope some Christians will hear the Bible's call to us to become good coyotes like, for instance, Jonah and Jesus.

Hearing Silenced Voices of the Bible: The "Other" Ten Commandments

If we are going to learn to listen to biblical border runners, we have to learn where to find them. If, upon learning about these biblical coyotes, your first thought was, OK, where are they? Why haven't I heard about them before? then you are not alone. In order to hear the voices for peace in the Bible, and especially the Old Testament, we have to learn to listen past the crowds of Christians over the centuries who have justified their cries for war and violence by using the scriptures. There may be crowds of them—but that does not make them right. "Majority rule" might be a good way to run a democratic state, but it can be a lousy way to read the Bible. If war and violence are the "normal way," then perhaps it is time to consider some "abnormal," or minority, ideas. So how do we read the minority voices in the Bible? Part of the task is learning to read in new ways, but another way is to learn to read "other" passages that have had little attention. In this book, we will explore the power of reading other passages in addition to well-known and popular passages.

Most Christians would agree that the Bible is the place to begin learning what it means to be a person of faith in the Christian tradition. It is, therefore, reasonable to presume that Christians ought to give serious time and effort to the study of the scriptures as a way of being open to the leading of God in our lives. But there can be some problems with reading the Bible when we read it to seek guidance in making ethical or faith decisions in our lives. One issue in particular presents itself. To put the matter bluntly: the Bible does not always speak with one voice on all issues of interest to modern readers. Christians have accepted for some time that there may be some differences between the Old Testament and the New Testament on some issues—after all, Jesus does begin some of his teaching by saying, "You have heard it said ... but I say ..." So what happens if it seems that the Bible provides diverse answers to the same question within the Old Testament itself? For example, Jehu believed that he had the blessing of God to massacre the descendants of Ahab in 2 Kings 10, yet the prophet Hosea raised serious questions about this brutality in Hosea 1:4-5. Another example is 1 Samuel 17, which describes the story of David killing Goliath, but 2 Samuel 21:19 doesn't seem to know that story and suggests that someone else killed the famous giant. Spotting the problem, the much later text in 1 Chronicles 20:5 tries to correct the discrepancy. Finally, some have argued the prophet Joel is more violent than Micah because Joel 3:10 reverses the famous "swords into plowshares" passage of Micah 4:3. Some Christians categorically deny that this kind of difference of perspective between portions of the Old Testament can ever happen, of course. The sad truth, however, is that many of us Christians deny these differences because we don't want to hear one of the voices: the one telling us to consider other ideas, or the voice telling us to cross borders. And so we read scripture just like we live our lives, silencing those who confront us with the inconvenient views of the strangers against whom we have drawn our border.

The problem of different voices in the Bible does not always arise with every issue of interest to modern Christians, but when it does arise, the problem is obvious, even if it is ignored by many Christian leaders who often would rather not deal with it. As it happens, however, the two general themes of this book—peacemaking and justice—are good examples to use for a discussion of this interesting problem.

On the issue of justice, it is arguably the case that there is very little variation within the scriptural record about what constitutes justice and righteousness, especially with regard to what it means to be concerned about each other as human beings. Why, then, do Christians have such differing ideas about what is "justice" in the Bible? One group of Christians in America, for example, strongly believes that copies of the Ten Commandments should be built into the actual walls of government courtrooms across the country, and they also argue that we should build more prisons and make marriage laws stronger. Other Christians wonder why churches do not do more to support labor unions, provide health care, and feed the hungry. Both can open their Bibles and go straight to verses supporting their views.

In the United States, even among those without a strong religious orientation, we also have competing ideas about "justice" that circulate among the general population. Police programs on TV portray victims of crimes "demanding justice." What we understand them to mean, of course, is "revenge," with the idea that "justice" means that something bad should happen to people who do bad things. Certainly the Bible speaks of punishment for those who violate community standards of behavior. As we will see, however, this punishment is not motivated in biblical ethics by seeking vengeance. Distorting *justice* to mean a socially acceptable way to demand *vengeance* has created some serious problems with how the Bible is read in North America.

In 2005, when the flood waters from Hurricane Katrina washed away any pretense in America that poverty was not as serious as it used to be, people also spoke of "justice" to mean access to the means of living—in other words, distribution of the economic and material benefits of American society includes assistance in times of trouble. In this case, "justice" would mean "equality" in some sense and especially some sense of equality of distributed necessities of life. There is a tendency, sadly typical of North American popular Christian thinking, that this equality only speaks of equal opportunity—as if we need not worry about what actually happens in society as long as we convince ourselves that everyone "had their chance" to live differently. This way, we can say to the poor, "It's your fault ... you had your chance like all the rest of us." Such talk is cruel, however, in a land that often features shamefully and unequally funded school districts and substandard facilities—not to speak of the home conditions of those in low-income or poverty areas. It is hard to imagine how many people actually do have an "equal chance," but in any case, it is interesting to note that the Bible features no thinking about justice as only an equal opportunity to have access to minimum economic or material needs. "Opportunity" is not a biblical issue—resulting social realities *are* a biblical issue. Of course, evil is not to be ignored or tolerated, and it *is* important that everyone have generally equal opportunities to make changes, but inequality in the *actual distribution* of economic and material means of life is a central biblical notion about "justice." Why isn't this more obvious in modern Christian faith and practice—especially among Christians in North America?

Contributing to the problem is our tendency to use one biblical voice to silence or ignore another. Since peacemaking and justice are interwoven concepts in the Bible, we can see the problem of ignored or silent voices in what the biblical laws—especially those in the Hebrew Bible (for Christians, the Old Testament)—have to say about justice. This is a good experiment, then, for learning to listen to other "voices" in the Bible, precisely because we think we have heard the biblical voice about justice clearly—especially when we hear the prophets or the Ten Commandments.

THE PROBLEM OF PROPHETIC ETHICS

When modern Christians think about justice, they invariably refer to the Hebrew prophets as sources of ethical thought to guide them. It is, of course, quite true that the books of the prophets are profound sources of inspiring thoughts about justice, especially the strong rhetoric of Amos, Micah, and Isaiah. While these prophets criticize the behavior of the ancient Israelites, more often than we care to admit they point out our problems as well. This is especially true when the prophetic books focus on the treatment of the poor and oppressed. It is important to notice how often the prophets refer to "the widow, the orphan, and the foreigner." These three categories of persons were the most vulnerable in ancient Israelite society—they were the easiest to forget, ignore, or exploit. Note that the following references cover over 250 years of prophetic activity among the Israelites, yet the theme is repeated again and again:

> **Isaiah 1:17:** Learn to do good; seek justice, rescue the oppressed, defend the orphan, plead for the widow.
>
> **Jeremiah 22:3:** Thus says the LORD: Act with justice and righteousness, and deliver from the hand of the oppressor anyone who has been robbed. And do no wrong or violence to the alien, the orphan, and the widow, or shed innocent blood in this place.
>
> **Ezekiel 22:7:** Father and mother are treated with contempt in you; the alien residing within you suffers extortion; the orphan and the widow are wronged in you.
>
> **Zechariah 7:10:** Do not oppress the widow, the orphan, the alien, or the poor; and do not devise evil in your hearts against one another.
>
> **Malachi 3:5:** Then I will draw near to you for judgment; I will be swift to bear witness against the sorcerers, against the adulterers, against those who swear falsely, against those who oppress the hired workers in their wages, the widow and the orphan, against those who thrust aside the alien, and do not fear me, says the LORD of hosts.

Furthermore, the prophets often point out that injustice is being practiced by those who outwardly claim to be religious and pious. Isn't it striking how often the prophets contrast impressive-looking religious practices with actually doing justice? Isaiah contrasts the pious practice of fasting with a "true fast":

Isaiah 58:5-8: Is such the fast that I choose, a day to humble one-self? Is it to bow down the head like a bulrush, and to lie in sack-cloth and ashes? Will you call this a fast, a day acceptable to the LORD? Is not this the fast that I choose: to loose the bonds of injus-tice, to undo the thongs of the yoke, to let the oppressed go free, and to break every yoke? Is it not to share your bread with the hungry, and bring the homeless poor into your house; when you see the naked, to cover them, and not to hide yourself from your own kin? Then your light shall break forth like the dawn, and your healing shall spring up quickly; your vindicator shall go before you, the glory of the LORD shall be your rear guard.

Micah contrasts the making of offerings against true repen-tance:

Micah 6:6-8: "With what shall I come before the LORD, and bow myself before God on high? Shall I come before him with burnt offerings, with calves a year old? Will the LORD be pleased with thousands of rams, with ten thousands of rivers of oil? Shall I give my firstborn for my transgression, the fruit of my body for the sin of my soul?" He has told you, O mortal, what is good; and what does the LORD require of you but to do justice, and to love kind-ness, and to walk humbly with your God?

Jeremiah condemns the pious practices of the Temple because the sacrifice is being offered by people who continue to do injustice:

Jeremiah 7:5-7: For if you truly amend your ways and your doings, if you truly act justly one with another, if you do not oppress the alien, the orphan, and the widow, or shed innocent blood in this place, and if you do not go after other gods to your own hurt, then I will dwell with you in this place, in the land that I gave of old to your ancestors forever and ever.

And Amos teaches that God will simply ignore the sacrifices of those who do not do justice:

Amos 5:21-24: I hate, I despise your festivals, and I take no delight in your solemn assemblies. Even though you offer me your burnt offerings and grain offerings, I will not accept them; and the offerings of well-being of your fatted animals I will not look upon. Take away from me the noise of your songs; I will not listen to the melody of your harps. But let justice roll down like waters, and righteousness like an ever-flowing stream.

Not only do the prophets condemn hypocritical piety, it is often the leaders who are the worst offenders. These are the leaders that were supposed to be guiding the ethical practices of the people of God:

Isaiah 10:1-2: Ah, you who make iniquitous decrees, who write oppressive statutes, to turn aside the needy from justice and to rob the poor of my people of their right, that widows may be your spoil, and that you may make the orphans your prey.

Micah 3:1-4: And I said: Listen, you heads of Jacob and rulers of the house of Israel. Should you not know justice?—you who hate the good and love the evil, who tear the skin off my people, and the flesh off their bones; who eat the flesh of my people, flay their skin off them, break their bones in pieces, and chop them up like meat in a kettle, like flesh in a caldron. Then they will cry to the LORD, but he will not answer them; he will hide his face from them at that time, because they have acted wickedly.

Micah 3:9-11: Hear this, you rulers of the house of Jacob and chiefs of the house of Israel, who abhor justice and pervert all equity, who build Zion with blood and Jerusalem with wrong. Its rulers give judgment for a bribe, its priests teach for a price, its prophets give oracles for money; yet they lean upon the Lord and say, "Surely the LORD is with us. No harm shall come upon us."

So, why is this section called "The Problem of Prophetic Ethics"? Surely the matter is clear: modern Christians should become more familiar with prophetic teachings that emphasize justice as well as religious practice, and the issues will begin to be dealt with. After all, if we say we want to be "biblical Christians"—the prophets are in the Bible too.

The problem is this—there really is no "prophetic ethic." The prophets arguably only seek to echo and reaffirm the Mosaic law and insist that the people of God live up to what God instructed "us" through Moses. Take, for example, the issue of the "widow, the orphan, and the foreigner/stranger/alien." What is common among these three? Note that the laws of Moses **already** insist on fair treatment for these three categories of person:

> **Exodus 22:22-23:** You shall not abuse any *widow* or *orphan*. If you do abuse them, when they cry out to me, I will surely heed their cry.

> **Deuteronomy 10:17-19:** For the LORD your God is God of gods and Lord of lords, the great God, mighty and awesome, who is not partial and takes no bribe, who executes justice for the *orphan* and the *widow,* and who loves the strangers, providing them food and clothing. You shall also love the stranger, for you were strangers in the land of Egypt.

The point is that in the Mosaic "legal system," widows, orphans, and aliens were particularly vulnerable because all land was distributed and owned among the mature male members of the tribes of Israel. It was, for better or worse, a patriarchal society, as most societies were in that region and time. The "Mosaic ideal," if we can call it that, was a generally equal distribution of land amongst the people—since land was the source of all income and well-being. But what if the male head-of-household dies? This is a serious matter if it is a young family with no mature males (although somewhat less serious if sons are ready to inherit land and carry on the family agricultural base—and it appears that in later biblical tradition, women could inherit the land). If left to their own, widows and orphans were vulnerable to serious abuse. What would they do for income? How would they live? Other males may try to take the land by ignoring or abusing the remaining family.

The answer is that the legal system of the Bible insisted that these widows and orphans be taken in by the nearest family members so that the young widowed family would have a home—at least until the heir to the father's land would be old enough to inherit. This was the situation in the book of Ruth—Naomi had to find the nearest relatives to help her and her Moabite daughter-in-law (cf. Leviticus 25). But what if the people did not take care of each other? What if they simply decided that they did not want to share and did not want to take on the financial burdens and responsibility for the needs of each other? As we shall see, there were actions that women could take to insist that near relatives do their duty.

Ignoring the weak in violation of the Mosaic ethics is precisely what the prophets bitterly condemn. The prophets teach us that people often do not care for the most vulnerable people of their society—however they got that way. What, then, about aliens? Why are they included? Because aliens were never part of the distribution system of Tribal Israel (in theory or in reality) they were also easily exploited—as the "foreigner" or "stranger" is always vulnerable in every society because they are the "other." So these three categories—widows, orphans, aliens—represent the weakest and the most vulnerable of ancient society. Care for the weakest of society was part of the biblical system of justice, including resident aliens.

So far, so good. So why don't we hear more from the churches about care for the modern equivalent of "the widow, the orphan, and alien"? It is not that we ignore the Bible itself, but rather that we only listen to part of it. Why did we talk about "prophetic ethics" when it was already in the Mosaic law? The answer is, I suggest, that most Christians know only a few Mosaic ethical teachings: ten as a matter of fact, and simply overlook or ignore many of the others. This, then, becomes a good example for learning to read passages that have often been silenced because they are uncomfortable.

IGNORING MOSES: TOO MUCH ABOUT THE TEN COMMANDMENTS?

Harper's Magazine reported that most American Christians (fully 75 percent) believe that the saying "God helps those who help themselves" occurs in the Bible. It does not; it comes from

Benjamin Franklin. This statistic is interesting in its relationship to the following questions: Why is the U.S. government the worst per capita provider of aid and assistance to other nations when compared to virtually all European nations? Why does this fact flatly contradict Americans' impression of ourselves as the most Christian nation in the world? Why do so many American Christians think that cutting taxes is more important than taking care of the weakest of our society by supporting medical care, welfare, schools, and other services? Why do so many of us think that paying for the latest military systems and hardware is far more important than taking care of "the widow, the orphan, and the foreigner"—while at the same time insisting that we, almost alone in the Christian world, truly believe the Bible to be God's Word?

The problem, I would suggest, is that we listen to a small part of Moses and ignore most of him. In so doing, we have unwittingly fulfilled Jesus' claim that, "If they do not listen to Moses and the prophets, neither will they be convinced even if someone rises from the dead" (Luke 16:31).

The point is that Christians **do** read about justice in the Bible. They read the Ten Commandments. It is virtually certain that the only portion of the Pentateuch's laws most "Bible-believing" Christians have read is the Ten Commandments. Why is that? Because so many of us believe that this is the only part of the laws of Moses we need pay any attention to, since Christians are "no longer under the law." That is, of course, until we need a verse to denounce homosexuality or another of our short list of "Really Big Sins," at which point we'll consult the entire Mosaic law with great vigor. But when it comes to the much more prominent teachings about social justice? Suddenly, then, Christians are "released from the law"—they are "no longer under the law, but under grace." How convenient. Quote it when you want … ignore it when it becomes uncomfortable.

There are other serious matters of biblical interpretation that have affected our views of justice in the Bible. When Christians speak as if they **do** deeply respect the ethical traditions of the

Bible, the "laws of Moses," they often believe that citing the Ten Commandments is basically a summary of the whole of the law. Now, it is true that as soon as one refers to the "laws of Moses" in modern Christian teaching and church life, it is widely presumed that we are speaking about the Ten Commandments. The Ten Commandments, in other words, have become a kind of short list, as if they represent the values of the Bible in a summary form. It is even popular to portray Moses carrying tablets with only these ten laws inscribed upon them. Is the widespread focus on the Ten Commandments by themselves, however, really a biblical idea?

Of course, these laws do appear—twice—in the Bible (Exodus 20 and Deuteronomy 5). But the question is not whether they are in the Bible or not—the problem is the nearly exclusive focus on the ten. There have always been scholars who wondered about the specific selection of the "ten words" as the tradition to focus on. Why these ten? Why not many other laws also discussed in the rest of the legal material? There are many important things about the Ten Commandments, of course. Reading through these laws, one gains a tremendous insight into the life of early Israel. It is not a complete picture, but we see what is valued—honesty, family integrity, property, and animals. You can't very well have a stable society without these moral values. So we can see that the Ten Commandments have social stability in mind. Now, I do believe that the Christian tradition, beginning already with Jesus, did determine that some laws are no longer binding on the followers of Jesus (or at the very least, of relative importance). Jesus' compassion leads us to overrule laws that seem cruel and severe in comparison with his teachings of love, for example. However, much of the compassion of Jesus' own teaching is *built* on major portions of the Mosaic tradition—the traditions far beyond the ten short verses we call "The Ten Commandments."

In recent years, however, some Christian scholars who study the Ten Commandments have made some interesting observations. Contrary to the tradition that suggests that these famous commandments were always intended to be taken as the timeless values out of the entire laws of Moses—values for all peoples at all times—some have argued that the Ten Commandments are rather limited in their scope and are especially intended for, perhaps even "targeted" toward, a particular part of the ancient Israelites.[1]

Try a little experiment. Read the Ten Commandments and then imagine who is being addressed. For example, since parents are mentioned, we presume that the person addressed has living parents. Since wives are mentioned, it is obviously a man being addressed. Since stealing is mentioned, the person obviously has some possessions, and so forth. One scholar, David Clines, somewhat humorously observes:

> Put together all the data we have in the commandments ... and what we find is: it is an individual, a male, an Israelite, employed, a house-owner, married, old enough to have working children but young enough to have living parents, living in a city, wealthy enough to possess an ox and an ass and slaves, important enough to be called to give evidence in a lawsuit. It is a man who is capable of committing, and probably tempted to commit, everything forbidden here—and likely to ignore everything enjoined here, if not commanded to observe it. It is, in short, one might say, a balding Israelite urban male with a mid-life crisis and a weight problem, in danger of losing his faith.[2]

Where is the voice of the poor? Where are the voices of the women, even the wives? The Ten Commandments do not even seem to address the royalty, the professional army, the merchant and trade classes, women, children, day laborers, and indentured servants. Instead, many have suggested that the Ten Commandments are the "middle class" commandments. It is not that they are bad laws—it is just that they are not whole and complete. They tend to speak to persons in certain limited social and economic circumstances. What about others? Are these the only real justice values of the Bible? Even worse, have we tended to prefer the Ten Commandments because they are useful to upwardly mobile, industrial Western "Christianized" societies (and their colonies)?

Have the Ten Commandments become so central in Western Christian traditions because we have come to value stable contracts (no false witnesses or lying), respect of property, and stable households (to enhance market economies and organized consumption) as the basic necessary values for economic development? Again, the problem is not the commandments themselves. After all, they are hardly debatable moral values in and of themselves—even if modern Christians quite rightly object to some of the language of the ancient laws (e.g., treating women as property).

I would argue, however, that it is a problem to focus on these ten as somehow central. To illustrate the problem, let us discuss what I have come to call the "Other Ten." Here are ten **other** Mosaic laws, from the same basic law codes where the more famous Ten Commandments are also found, except that these "Other Ten" tend to illustrate rather different social and economic values. These are not special laws, nor are they found together one after the other (although most of them are quite closely grouped in Deuteronomy), but I have chosen them to specifically illustrate quite different ideas about what justice in the Bible also means:

The Other Ten:

(1) Leviticus 25—The law of Jubilee

(2) Deuteronomy 22:8—Building railings on upper floors

(3) Deuteronomy 23:24-25—The right to eat in a neighbor's field

(4) Deuteronomy 20—Soldiers must have experienced the blessings of peace before becoming warriors

(5) Deuteronomy 24:14—On the wages of the poor

(6) Deuteronomy 24:17—On justice for resident aliens

(7) Deuteronomy 24:19—The right of gleaning grapes and olives

(8) Deuteronomy 25:13—On punishment that is not degrading

(9) Deuteronomy 25:5-10—The rights of childless widows

(10) Deuteronomy 23:15-16—The right of refuge for economic slaves

Let us examine each of the Other Ten briefly.

(1) Leviticus 25—The Law of Jubilee

Included in this chapter is the notion that every fifty years, the Year of Jubilee is proclaimed, and all land that has been leased to wealthier Israelites returns to the original tribal owners who possessed it, under the ideal of more equal distribution of land. If an Israelite farmer falls into debt, he can lease his land to wealthier Israelites. But this is not supposed to be permanent. It is only supposed to last until the original family is economically back on its feet. To be certain that such land distribution does not start to favor only the wealthy, the priests of ancient Israel instituted the Jubilee to return leased land back to the original families.

The idea of the Year of Jubilee is simple—give succeeding generations another chance, so they are not condemned by the economic mistakes (or unforeseen problems) of previous generations. In other words, there should not be a rampant problem of the inheritance of poverty among the poor, as well as the rich inheriting entirely unearned wealth and creating permanent advantages for some people. Where are "equal opportunities" in that kind of society?

Whenever I speak on this subject, invariably someone cynically asks me if this was "ever really practiced." This is an interesting question for biblical ethics, when you think about it. Americans rarely, for example, ask if capital punishment in old Mosaic laws was ever "really practiced." Nor do they ask such questions of the Ten Commandments, for example, where it is presumed that they were practiced. The implication is that somehow this is not a real law, but the Ten Commandments are real.

In fact, most biblical scholars think that Leviticus 25 is among later biblical laws introduced by the priests after the Exile to try and deal with the abuses practiced by the elite and the Monarchy before the Exile. The strong likelihood of this is supported by the fact that the priest-prophet Ezekiel provides his own variation on the Jubilee distribution system in his vision for restored Israel (Ezekiel 40–48). Here, Ezekiel specifically condemns the wealthy elite and the monarchy, the "shepherds," for their hoarding of land and causing oppression. In the midst of his redistribution system, Ezekiel pauses to clarify why any future monarch's land will be limited and why the wealthy elite will have to live with honest measures so that they can no longer cheat the people:

> **Ezekiel 45:8b-10a:** And my princes shall no longer oppress my people; but they shall let the house of Israel have the land according to their tribes. Thus says the Lord GOD: Enough, O princes of Israel. Put away violence and oppression, and do what is just and right. Cease your evictions of my people, says the Lord GOD. You shall have honest balances.

From this point on, Ezekiel continues to describe his version of the land redistribution system that echoes the Jubilee concept in Leviticus 25. According to the values of this "commandment," justice in the Bible involves reasonable distribution of the basics of life—including the opportunity for people to work, have enough, and have stable economic lives. Curious, then, that when we read in church the passages like Leviticus 25, or Ezekiel 45, we are doing something we call "Bible study," yet when peasants in Latin America or Africa speak of "redistributing land," they are called "troublemakers" and are declared dangerous by the World Bank. Perhaps both are right—biblical law can be revolutionary.

(2) Deuteronomy 22:8—Building railings on upper floors

This is simple and straightforward. Israelites are responsible for hazards in their buildings. Thus, biblical law has an ancient "Building and Safety Code," and, therefore, yet another level of care of the "other" that may seem to some Americans as an infringement on personal freedoms. Indeed it does limit personal freedom, but according to the Mosaic ethic, personal freedoms do not include creating hazards for others.

(3) Deuteronomy 23:24-25—The right to eat in a neighbor's field

The poor in ancient Israel had the right to feed themselves in your fields. They could not harvest anything (put anything in a container), but they could eat. This was not considered stealing, it seems, unless the food was carried out of the field in some kind of container. This speaks of providing for the basic needs of life— not merely the opportunity to work. The Bible, therefore, states that the poor have a right to a modest portion of what God provides to the rest of us.

(4) Deuteronomy 20—Military exemptions

In this fascinating passage, soldiers are released from active duty for reasons we do not always think about, if they have started a garden, built a house without living in it, or have become engaged. What is interesting about these three things is that they are signs of stable life. To live under "your own vine and fig tree" (Zech. 3:10) is considered among the blessings of peace. The clear implication of this is that potential soldiers must have experienced the blessings of peace before becoming warriors. Yet, in many modern societies, soldiers are drawn from the poor, the minorities, and sometimes even the foreigners. It is the wealthy who are defended by the poor. Soldiers from poorer backgrounds, we try to say, are given opportunities and training that they can use in their lives. That is, of course, if they survive the wars in which they defend the wealthy. These biblical laws are intended to prevent just exactly what has happened in many developed countries—a class difference in creating poor warriors to defend wealthy elite.

(5) Deuteronomy 24:14—On the wages of the poor

Laborers would often be outside one's own family, perhaps aliens. Here is one of the ways in which the aliens could be exploited: by withholding wages. In modern American practice, it has often occurred that alien farm workers from Mexico and other developing Latin nations are worked in the fields and then conveniently discovered to be aliens and summarily deported before receiving their pay. This is tantamount to slavery.

Deuteronomy 24 prevents such withholding of wages because the people are reminded that they were once slaves in Egypt, and the poor workers might "cry out to God" just like the Israelite slaves did (Deut. 24:15). Frequently, the biblical laws point out that Israel will begin to act like Egyptian oppressors. Their very insistence on a King, for example, is compared to Egyptian enslavement (1 Samuel 8). Furthermore, it is arguable that *substandard wages* are equally a violation of withholding wages.

(6) Deuteronomy 24:17—On justice for resident aliens

Not only is it possible to withhold wages, but it is also possible to corrupt the justice system so that the poor wage earners have nowhere to turn. Then the Israelites are acting like an oppressive Pharaoh, and God will hear the cries of the oppressed. Even the alien may appeal to God (like Hagar the Egyptian in the wilderness, who appealed to God; cf. Genesis 21).

(7) Deuteronomy 24:19—The right of gleaning grapes and olives

This law is related to number 3 above, but now allows a minor "harvesting" of the remainders of olive groves and grapevines after the owners have taken their main harvest. Owners of such fields are not to harvest every last bit that they can—they must leave a portion for the poor. This portion is the right of the people, especially the poor and the hungry. Those who argue that in the modern world all working people are entitled to keep every penny that they earn without regard to the poor ("welfare") are simply engaging in a nonbiblical greed that has nothing to do with Christian or biblical faith.

(8) Deuteronomy 25:13—On punishment that is not degrading

This would seem a strange law to regard highly in the modern world, but I think that it is interesting and significant. I do not agree with lashing as a serious form of punishment, of course, but within the ancient context, this law has an interesting component to it—punishment of evil is allowed, but there is a principle involved in how that punishment is to be selected. Your "brother" must not be "degraded in your sight." The term "degraded" is used also in Deuteronomy 27:16 as "dishonor" and in Isaiah 3:5 as "insolent":

> **Deuteronomy 27:16:** "Cursed be anyone who dishonors father or mother."

> **Isaiah 3:5:** The people will be oppressed, everyone by another and everyone by a neighbor; the youth will be insolent to the elder, and the base to the honorable.

The principle for modern thinking is not that punishment ought not to exist—it arguably should in some form—but that whatever punishment is believed to be necessary must never **degrade** a fellow human being. Lashing, of course, would be considered degrading today, but it is amazing how quickly we abandon standards of decency when we believe that torture or severity are called for, such as the treatment of POWs in U.S.-run camps in Guantanamo Bay and elsewhere. It is rather obvious that modern ideas about punishment often abandon any thought of the humanity of the criminal, or we would not have the kind of prison system that dehumanizes other human beings. I do not speak here of abandoning the need for a modern concept of criminal justice, but Christians must insist that criminal justice maintain human dignity, or they abandon the Bible.

(9) Deuteronomy 25:5-10—The rights of childless widows

We spoke earlier of the weakness of the widow, orphan, and alien. It is an interesting aspect of biblical law that widows can be provided with heirs to their family land by the next male relative actually engaging in sexual intercourse with her and providing her with a child. The technical term for this is levirate marriage. Why would a brother or near male relative refuse to provide a female relative with an heir in this way? Many modern readers may think of the sexual ethics involved and cringe at this idea, of course, but in ancient society, it is not because of some sexual modesty on his part. It is because if a female relative has no son, the living male relative could inherit the widow's land to himself, free and clear (cf. Gen. 38:8-9). So, the Mosaic laws give the widow a fascinating right—the public humiliation of the man who refuses to provide for her future economic well-being. The issue here is not sexual, the issue is providing for the economically disadvantaged. It is not too far, therefore, to point out that feminist protest in behalf of women's rights, beginning with the right to vote and total enfranchisement and including full equality for women in all levels of religious leadership, are the biblical rights of women throughout the world. Public humiliation of male greed is a biblical right, especially where the economic well-being of women is involved.

(10) Deuteronomy 23:15-16—The right of refuge for economic slaves

What is called slavery throughout most of the Bible (foreign slaves were exceedingly rare) is the economic practice that today is referred to as indentured servitude. We are speaking here of a seven-year period of work to repay debts. Be that as it may, in American history we know that some Christians actually defended slavery from the Bible using those passages referring to indentured servitude—but this was clearly a selective process—taking scissors to their Bibles in a manner that would have made Jefferson proud. (Jefferson, of course, famously clipped out portions of his Bible that he did not like. It seems that ignoring uncomfortable passages is an old American tradition.) Had this passage, our tenth "Other Law," become American law, slavery would have had a very short time span, as it would have been the legal right of slaves to simply walk away when abused. Secondly, it is clear that the system envisioned in the Bible was intended to be so humane that indentured servants were to be treated with justice or the "deal was off." As employment today can often amount to indentured servitude under modern American economic rules, it is equally clear that protests, walk-outs, and union organizing for decent treatment and wages are quite clearly within biblical concepts of justice.

Why not observe these "Other Ten" in our understanding of biblical justice? There is little mystery surrounding the virtual ignoring of these and many, many other laws equally interesting and often equally relevant to the modern Christian church. Of course, I chose these ten to illustrate a very important central point—the totality of biblical law presumes a definition of justice that includes a notion of distribution of resources in a very basic sense. Biblical law does not replace the need for modern Christians to do serious thinking about modern economic and political systems and their roles within those systems. What it does provide, however, are basic principles that guide our notion of what it is that we must work toward. Christian political activism cannot stop at simply advocating equal opportunity and then taking a back seat and letting the "chips fall where they may," putting the blame of laziness or bad fortune on anyone who is not successful and well off. Such thinking is deeply part of the American mind-set, and it is entirely antagonistic to the Mosaic ideal of justice, which provides the foundational values for prophetic preaching.

My basic observation is this: not all biblical laws can easily apply to modern Christian thinking about justice. But, we ought not easily silence all other laws outside the Ten Commandments where far more radical social justice expectations are outlined, especially when we have very little basis for deciding that the "Ten" are the only ones we must pay attention to. We cannot "silence the other voice."

Modern Christians and the "Other Ten"

The principles that we have articulated in our "Other Ten Commandments" can be translated into modern values that can guide modern Christian activism:

(1) Equitable distribution of resources to all humans—everyone has the right to the basic necessities of life.
(2) People have a responsibility for their actions and the potential ill effects of their actions on others.
(3) People have a right to expect our help from our resources.

Everything we earn from our work does not belong completely and entirely to ourself.

(4) Among the evils of modern war is the fact that war has become part of an economically oppressive system of maintaining power and privilege—the poor warrior is paid to defend the privileges of the elite.

(5) The wage earner must be paid. The modern Fair Trade movement is a deeply biblical notion of pressuring modern production to fairly compensate the workers for the true value of their work—not the minimum that we can get away with and still keep workers alive and standing at the assembly lines.

(6) The same is true for "foreign workers" who are often imported quietly, exploited, and then deported with great fanfare.

(7) The more well-known Ten Commandments say, "Do not steal." But it is obviously not "stealing" when the poor insist on some minimum support. It is their right to expect to have some basic benefits from the economic production of a society.

(8) Modern stable societies depend on segregating criminals from wider society. It is to be presumed that, even after a more equitable distribution of resources cuts deeply into criminal behaviors, there will remain the social deviants who engage in criminal behavior that is destructive to society. There is a place for punishment—even if it means permanent segregation of criminals from wider society. But this is to be guided by humane treatment, not degrading behavior. Victims' rights do not include dehumanizing vengeance.

(9) Women and other members of oppressed peoples have a right to bring their oppression to public attention in order that justice may be done. It is not merely that they have the right to protest—this is not a matter of freedom of speech. It is the right to publicly protest **with the expectation that justice will be restored**.

(10) Anyone who is abused in their workplace or in their homes has the right of refuge. There is no right of employer or family head that allows abuse or mistreatment. Abused workers can leave. Abused spouses can leave.

What have these Other Ten to do with Jesus? Quite a bit, really. These ten must be included in any basic evaluation of the heritage within which Jesus stands as Messiah and Lord. Jesus arguably asserts precisely these kinds of values as basic to his teaching. We need not go into great detail—each and every one of these Other Ten Mosaic values of justice can be compared to the life and teachings of Jesus (and the early followers like Paul) such as noting the following examples:

Jesus exercises his right of public humiliation of elites by his "cleansing of the Temple" episode (Mark 11; Matthew 21; Luke 19; John 2); Jesus insists that participation in his movement precedes and supercedes family obligations and "rights of employers" (the meaning of his "sword" that divides families—Matt. 10:34ff). Jesus speaks of visiting those in prison and thus acknowledging their humanity (Matthew 25). Jesus speaks of sharing from one's wealth as deeply essential to being a part of his movement (Matthew 25). Paul considers sharing with poorer Christians to be essential (Rom. 15:26ff). Jesus condemns the abuse of the foreigner by honoring Samaritans—the hated "other" who lived among the Jews (Luke 10; John 4—and Jesus is even **called** a "Samaritan" for doing so—John 8). Jesus insists on the rights of the poor to have basic necessities according to the Mosaic Law (Matt. 5:6; Mark 10:21; Luke 14:12-14). Even when Judas is told to "go do what you must do" with the disciples' money, the disciples presume Jesus is sending him to give to the poor (John 13:27-29). Jesus teaches that providing restitution to exploited workers is righteousness (Luke 19:8). And we could go on.

This experiment in reading other laws as well as the Ten Commandments illustrates a central principle of reading the Bible: sometimes we must look at other voices, even minority ones, to gain a clearer understanding of biblical teaching on issues of great significance. This is especially the case when the issue is war and peacemaking.

NONVIOLENT JUSTICE: JUSTICE THAT VIOLATES BORDERS

Let us now return to the basic theme of this book: I have argued that making peace and doing justice can often involve violating borders. What are these borders? In the ancient as well as the modern world, people have constructed borders to separate themselves from others. Whether these are geographical borders of nation-states or the borders between certain social groups or economic classes, too many people in the modern Christian world believe that borders are necessary to preserve privilege and privileged identities.

Modern discussions of biblical justice tend to focus on those "within the border" of membership in ancient Israel. However, when we deal with "the nations" in the Old Testament, we more typically speak of those who stand on the other side of borders that have been created. Justice is, therefore, often considered to be for the individual alien who is "within our borders," or "among you," not over there among "the nations." Reading the Hebrew Bible, one could easily get the impression that there is a difference in biblical ethics between neighbors and "the nations." ("Nations" in this case meaning "other peoples besides us.")

The Old Testament often speaks about borders between "them" and "us." There is a clear difference between just treatment of the foreigner "amongst us," and "the nations" beyond. There are famous lists of "enemy nations" (Exod. 3:8, 17; 23:23; Deut. 7:1; 20:17; etc.) that continued to be used even in books written very late in pre-Christian history (Judith 5:16). There were even racist slurs. Note the use of "you son of Canaanites" in the story of Susanna, the late Greek addition to the book of Daniel (Susanna 1:56). Israelites were counseled against associating with foreigners of neighboring kingdoms (Deut. 23:3), and thus "mixed marriages" were to be avoided, according to Ezra 9 and 10, and 1 Kings 11:1-2 implies that King Solomon's downfall was partly because of his love of foreign women in mixed marriages. These tendencies toward hatred and rejection do exist—some ancient Hebrews thought this way. But not all of them....

At the same time, however, the Old Testament books frequently allude to violating the borders of Israelite identity. Not only have we seen the calls for justice for the resident aliens but also we will see that there are many such violations of the borders that are presented in the biblical record, often in the name of peacemaking and doing justice.

In the chapters that follow, I present a rather simple thesis. I argue that the basis for the Christian opposition to violence and warfare actually has its roots in the Old Testament. Although biblical nonviolence finds its most unambiguous Hebraic expression in Jesus, the Bible's criticism of violence derives in the first instance from the willingness of some Old Testament writers to violate human borders and extend the expectations of justice beyond our own narrowly defined group or tribe. It comes from the expectation that we will treat "them" as though they were part of "us." When we put it this way, of course, it begins to sound rather familiar—something about treating others the way we would like to be treated.

I will further argue that the biblical case against warfare is rooted, not primarily in a biblical critique of violence (which invariably ends up contrasting the "peaceful Jesus" with the supposedly "vengeful Old Testament"), but rather in the biblical understanding of violating separations. In the Bible justice extends to the "other people"—even to the enemy—and thus holds out the possibility of their transformation by conversion (in mission) or becoming a coexisting human partner (in dialogue). To put it another way, biblical nonviolence is rooted in the "Old Testament" courage of a Hebrew minority willing to violate the borders of the majority. Any Christians who try to limit their compassion and struggle for justice to "our people," "our citizens," or even "fellow Christians" have betrayed these Hebrew voices, and ultimately, the voice of Jesus as well. Jesus is the ultimate violator of our human borders. Jesus is an embodiment of the good coyote. He stands in the tradition of other Old Testament coyotes who ran borders long before our Messiah arrived on the earth to show us how this border running is really done—and did so in a way impossible to ignore.

Violent Times and Courageous Hopes: A History of Two Biblical Wars, 587 BCE and 70 CE

THE VIOLENT CONTEXT OF BIBLICAL BORDERS

In order to trace a history of faithful "illegals" or "border violators" in the Bible, we should first acknowledge that violence in biblical history often gave rise to new thinking about establishing borders and violating borders. This seems entirely rational—we have already observed that violence is typically the ultimate expression of creating human borders, and at the same time, the most powerful means of maintaining those borders. Sometimes these boundaries are geographical. Other times they are ideological, religious, racial, or cultural. Always they are human creations.

The most famous "border violators" of the Christian Bible (including Jonah and Jesus) arise in the context of the ultimate expression of human borders—warfare. Therefore, I suggest that a great deal of the Bible ought to be read in the context of two great acts of international violence that had a transformative impact on the people of God and the book they left for us: the fall of Jerusalem in 587 BCE and the fall of Jerusalem again in 70 CE. While many other major events relevant to the biblical ideas of peace and justice occurred along the way, our purposes will be best served if we orient ourselves for a time to these two critical, violent episodes. In fact, we are following contemporary trends in biblical scholarship by highlighting these two violent episodes of biblical history as centrally important "watershed events" for understanding most of the biblical texts, both Old and New Testaments.

The first critical event is the Babylonian Exile, which involved the destruction of Jerusalem (and Solomon's Temple) by the Babylonians 587 years before the time of Jesus. This devastating event not only had a clear impact on the Hebrew people but also the most formative impact on the shape of the Old Testament. This is somewhat ironic, given that the more well-known event of the Old Testament for most Christians is the Exodus story. If the Exodus events, according to biblical tradition, led to the formation and creation of the Hebrew people, the Babylonian Exile resulted in a radical **reformulation of** the identity of God's people. After the Exile, the Hebrew people had to redefine themselves as a people without king, land, or army. It raised serious questions about the future: Should we try to regain our national identity? Or should we define ourselves as another kind of "people" of God? It was questions like these that led to a debate about what it means to be God's people. This debate arguably continued well into the New Testament period as well, and in many ways these same questions are an important aspect of the second great act of violence: the Jewish Revolt of 70 CE and the horrific Roman response. Like the Babylonian Exile for the Old Testament period, the violent Roman response was the major watershed for New Testament history. Let's start with the first crisis before considering the second.

The first event we are interested in is relatively easy to summarize:[1] Almost six hundred years before the time of Jesus, King Nebuchadnezzar—the ruler of the Babylonian Empire—conquered Jerusalem and the surrounding land of Judah. This was the last independent Hebrew nation in the ancient world. There were once two Hebrew nations after Solomon's death, circa 922 BCE—one in the north (Israel) and in the south (Judah). The northern kingdom of Israel, however, fell to the Assyrian Empire in

722 BCE, more than 125 years before the southern kingdom of Judah faced the Babylonian armies. We know from historical records that the Babylonian soldiers would often round up the upper classes of the population they conquered and exile their entire families back into the empire's heartland. This tactic was to prevent resistance or revolts, but there is some suggestion that it served Babylonian economic interests as well. Let us try to spell out some of the wider implications of this conquest and exile.

The Babylonian conquest of Jerusalem was the end of the series of crises in this region. As we noted, the monarchy ended for the northern kingdom of Israel in 722, and the remaining southern kingdom of Judah was devastated in two steps—when Jerusalem surrendered to a Babylonian siege in 597, and then tried to revolt and was subsequently destroyed in 587.

Most of the battles of the Bible were not open-field battles between armies but rather siege warfare involving walled cities. But we should make no mistake about one historical reality of war in the biblical era: siege warfare was dreadful.[2] When city walls were finally breached, looting, burning, massacres, as well as taking prisoners, were almost always the results.

When the Babylonian regime first arose, it faced the challenge of defeating what remained of the mighty Assyrian Empire, which had ruled throughout the ancient Near East with an iron fist for centuries.[3] In 609, the last Assyrians fell to the rising Babylonian forces, and Nebuchadnezzar began to entertain ambitions to control Egypt as well. This required controlling the land bridge between the territories he controlled and the lands of Egypt. As usual in the ancient Near East, part of this land bridge was ancient Palestine. Nebuchadnezzar eventually controlled this territory in 598/7. At that point, young King Jehoiachin of Judah surrendered (2 Kings 24–25). According to Nebuchadnezzar's own inscriptions, he appointed in Jerusalem, "a king of his own liking, took heavy booty from it, and brought it into Babylon."[4]

According to 2 Kings 24:14, the number of exiles taken at this time was 10,000, but added in 2 Kings 24:16 is that 7,000 artisans and 1,000 smiths were also taken, for a total of 18,000. This compares to Jeremiah 52:28, which notes 3,023 persons carried into captivity. Scholars have debated which number is more reliable, or whether they measure different areas conquered, and even whether this number counts only men.

The new ruler, Zedekiah, tried to revolt in the eleventh year of Nebuchadnezzar. This revolt led to Nebuchadnezzar's return to reassert control, and the Babylonian armies laid siege to the city in 587/6. On August 5, 587 (or August 15, 586), the city fell to Nebuchadnezzar's siege, and Zedekiah's resistance was crushed. Zedekiah was captured at Jericho and his sons were brutally killed before his eyes. Then his eyes were put out before he was taken "in fetters" (2 Kings 25:7) to Babylon. Babylonian control over Palestine lasted from 597 through 539, when the imperial control of Palestine changed from Babylonian to Persian rule. In the most recent overview of the archaelogical and biblical data on the exilic events, the Israeli scholar Oded Lipshits has summarized the impact of the exile. He writes: "The first conclusion that arises from the survey data is that between the Iron Age and the Persian Period there was a sharp decline—more than 90%—in occupation in the environs of Jerusalem."[5] Lipshits concludes: "The demographic evidence thus supports the previous hypothesis that Jerusalem remained desolate throughout the time of Babylonian Rule." In fact, Lipshits estimates that the total population of Judah at the end of the Iron Age was 108,000 (that is, before the exilic events occurred) and at the beginning of the Persian Period drops down to 30,125. He observes: "It appears that the destruction of Jerusalem and the end of the Kingdom of Judah brought about the gravest demographic crisis in the history of the Kingdom of Judah."[6]

However, the Neo-Babylonian regime came to an end with legendary swiftness (Isaiah 45). Cyrus the Persian ruler, after unifying the Persian tribes and defeating the Medes, conquered the city of Babylon in 539. What we now refer to as "The Persian Period" of biblical history extends from 539 to the conquests of Alexander the Great in circa 333 BCE. The biblical sources about the early Persian period indicate that the Persians were initially understood to be generous liberators in their return of some of the exiles to their homelands, including the Jews. However, recent work on the Persian period reveals that this supposed enlightened rule of the Persians (including Cyrus) can be greatly exaggerated and Nehemiah 9:36-37 gives an entirely darker picture of the later Persian rule over the Jews in Palestine. As we can see throughout history, one of the cruelties of outside military interference is that such intervention often creates conditions of internal instability in the invaded territories. Under such intense pressures, societies often break down, and family violence, feuding, and factionalism is clearly visible. In fact, the Bible reveals examples of this kind of internal instability under pressure.

THE DAMAGE TO ISRAELITE COMMUNITIES AND FAITH

It is difficult to estimate the extent of what we would today call the humanitarian crises of 597 and 587, but archaeological and biblical evidence begins to draw a picture of horrific events that become permanently etched into the historical memory of the Hebrew Bible (e.g., Psalm 137; Lamentations). Jerusalem and the Temple were destroyed. The people who were taken as exiles must have lived with severe limitations on their movement and economic life. Nebuchadnezzar's own inscriptions bragged that he put many of the deported peoples to work.

Recent evidence reveals that the exiles were settled in separate communities, which at least allowed them to maintain some kind of communal identity. The available evidence, which isn't plentiful in the Bible or outside the Bible, nevertheless paints a picture of their life in dark colors, even if we must carefully work with the use of metaphors and allusions rather than precise historical observation. For example, the biblical discussions of the time of exile includes terms like chains and bonds, which may be symbolic images but they are certainly not symbolic of ease and light treatment (Isa. 52:2; Lam. 3:7). Psalms from this time speak of "darkness and gloom" (107:14). Other passages compare the exile to "imprisonment" (Jer. 32:2; Isa. 43:6; etc.). The opening lines of Psalm 137 are often cited to express dreary life in exile:

Psalm 137:1-5: By the rivers of Babylon—there we sat down and there we wept when we remembered Zion. On the willows there we hung up our harps. For there our captors asked us for songs, and our tormentors asked for mirth, saying, "Sing us one of the songs of Zion!" How could we sing the LORD's song in a foreign land? If I forget you, O Jerusalem, let my right hand wither!

Life would have been difficult for the Hebrews left back in the land as well. A wealth of archaeological evidence paints a stark picture of life in Palestine after the tragedies of the Babylonian conquest in 587 BCE. Writing a popular article on "The Fury of Babylon," archaeologist and historian Lawrence Stager refers to the "scorched-earth" policy of the Neo-Babylonian Empire that created "a veritable wasteland west of the Jordan River."[7]

If one turns to Lamentations there is evidence for depressing conditions back in Palestine. The rubble of destroyed buildings is referred to (2:2), and in 5:2-5 especially, there is strong suggestion of regimented economic activity in the land:

Lamentations 5:2-5: Our inheritance has been turned over to strangers, our homes to aliens. We have become orphans, father-less; our mothers are like widows. We must pay for the water we drink; the wood we get must be bought. With a yoke on our necks we are hard driven; we are weary, we are given no rest.

Violence in the area suggests lawlessness and danger from brigands:

Lamentations 5:9, 11: We get our bread at the peril of our lives, because of the sword in the wilderness.... Women are raped in Zion, virgins in the towns of Judah.

There even seems to be tension between the groups taken as prisoners of war and those Hebrews who remained back in the devastated land. Second Chronicles claims that religious life vir-tually ended back in Palestine, but this is usually seen as an exag-gerated view, possibly motivated by the serious divisions between the people who were taken as exiles (many of whom later returned to try to rebuild their lives) and those who remained back in the land throughout this entire era. There is further evidence of such conflicts between the exiles and those left in the land, as evident in the book of Ezekiel. The conflict suggests organized life in both locations as well as deeply divided ideas about who now possesses the remaining land (e.g., Ezek. 33:23-29; compare the "good" versus "bad" figs in Jer. 24:1-10). This tension is probably behind the breakout of anger and resentments when some of the prisoners of war return home after Cyrus conquers Babylon, as described in chapters 1–6 of Ezra. There, a conflict broke out on the question of who, in fact, was authorized by the Persians to rebuild the Temple (and thus control the important economic exchanges that were also based at the Temple)—people who had remained in the land or recent returnees from exile. Destruction, social disruption, religious crisis—the exile is rightly understood to be the single most devastating challenge to the Hebrew people in biblical history.

THE THEOLOGICAL CHANGES FROM THE EXILE

So why is all this important? Granted that life went through severe changes in the Babylonian Exile, didn't the exile end? Apparently not. Even after the Greek period begins after Alexander the Great's conquests (333 BCE), and probably as late as circa 165 BCE, the book of Daniel recalculates the years of exile to be 480 years instead of Jeremiah's predicted seventy years (see Jeremiah 29). Daniel multiplies this by seven. In other words—the writer of Daniel centuries after 587 still believes that an "exile" continues (Dan. 9:24-27). Finally, in the New Testament, the Epistle of 1 Peter addresses itself to "the exiles of the dispersion" in 1:1 and finishes with a reference to "your sister church in Babylon" (5:13). Exilic symbolism was still deeply meaningful to the early Christian communities as well, centuries later than 587 BCE.

What do we conclude? The Exile was a watershed event in the life of the biblical people. No longer would questions of war and peace be asked in the same way, with the same meaning. It is one thing to debate issues of war and peace if we are thinking about an Israelite monarchy with kings, armies, and the money to equip them. But after the Exile, the people must ask new questions: what does it mean to be the people of God in these new circumstances?

An interesting hint at these new questions is a fascinating passage in Proverbs (a collection of wise sayings written soon after the horrific events that started the Exile) that seems to raise these new questions in a series of animal images:

> **Proverbs 30:24-28:** Four things on earth are small, yet they are exceedingly wise: the ants are a people without strength, yet they provide their food in the summer; the badgers are a people without power, yet they make their homes in the rocks; the locusts have no king, yet all of them march in rank; the lizard can be grasped in the hand, yet it is found in kings' palaces.

These are interesting illustrations. What is particularly interesting, however, is that in each case, the animals represent the condition of the Hebrew people after 587 BCE. They were without strength, without king, and without power, yet they had spread throughout the empire. This passage raises a central question (some may argue **the** central question) of post–587 BCE biblical thought: just what does it mean to be the people of God *now?* For some biblical writers, it was obviously a time to think in radically new ways—such as a redefined sense of mission to the rest of the world activated by a vision to be God's instruments of peace and justice for all peoples (e.g., Isa. 2:2-4; Isa. 19:24-25; and especially Isa. 49:6).

THE BIBLICAL DEBATE IN THE EXILIC PERIOD

A debate takes place between biblical books (and sometimes within a single biblical book) over this question of what it means to be the people of God now, when one is living in the shadow of Exile or in the diaspora, living away from the old homeland. A related, and equally interesting, question also presents itself. If we must rethink who we are, must we not also rethink who *the nations* are? In other words, for many having a clear identity requires the establishment of clear borders: borders that serve to identify the difference between "friend and foe," "us and them." Yet the Exile has thrown those borders into chaos. With regard to both of these questions, then—"who are we?" as God's people, and "who are they?" as *the nations*—there are signs of intense debate after the time of the Exile.

The best example of this debate within the Bible is to cite an *actual* debate—the face-off between the prophets Jeremiah and Hananiah. The biblical text portrays Hananiah and Jeremiah each trying to influence Zedekiah, the interim ruler placed by the Babylonians in Jerusalem between 597–587. (In other words, after the surrender of Jerusalem to Babylon but before the final destruction of Jerusalem in 587.) According to Jeremiah chapter 28, Hananiah presents his argument first:

Jeremiah 28:2-4: Thus says the LORD of hosts, the God of Israel: I have broken the yoke of the king of Babylon. Within two years I will bring back to this place all the vessels of the LORD's house, which King Nebuchadnezzar of Babylon took away from this place and carried to Babylon ... for I will break the yoke of the king of Babylon.

But Jeremiah did not agree. Jeremiah believed that Babylon was the tool being used by God to fulfill the threats in passages like Jeremiah 7 and also the fulfillment of passages like Deuteronomy 28:

Deuteronomy 28:47-50: Because you did not serve the LORD your God joyfully and with gladness of heart for the abundance of everything, therefore you shall serve your enemies whom the LORD will send against you, in hunger and thirst, in nakedness and lack of everything. He will put an iron yoke on your neck until he has destroyed you. The LORD will bring a nation from far away, from the end of the earth, to swoop down on you like an eagle, a nation whose language you do not understand, a grim-faced nation showing no respect to the old or favor to the young.

Using the same imagery of the iron yoke, Jeremiah reports:

Jeremiah 28:14: For thus says the LORD of hosts, the God of Israel: I have put an iron yoke on the neck of all these nations so that they may serve King Nebuchadnezzar of Babylon, and they shall indeed serve him; I have even given him the wild animals.

It is particularly interesting, however, to note that Jeremiah even suggested that God had plans for the exiles and that they were not to revolt or resist (as Hananiah had hoped):

Jeremiah 29:4-7: Thus says the LORD of hosts, the God of Israel, to all the exiles whom I have sent into exile from Jerusalem to Babylon: Build houses and live in them; plant gardens and eat what they produce. Take wives and have sons and daughters; take wives for your sons, and give your daughters in marriage, that they may bear sons and daughters; multiply there, and do not decrease. But seek the welfare of the city where I have sent you into exile, and pray to the LORD on its behalf, for in its welfare you will find your welfare.

Notice that the three images of building houses, planting gardens, and getting married are the three "exemptions" from fighting a war in Deuteronomy 20. It seems beyond doubt that Jeremiah not only opposed any revolt against Babylon but also insisted that the exiles may have a positive impact during their time of exile as well by seeking *shalom=welfare* of the city where God sent them. Jeremiah effectively redefines what it means to be the people of God in these circumstances and disagrees with the notion that being the people of God must only be about power, authority, and land—or even destruction of enemies.

To summarize, the devastation of the exile created partisan struggles, infighting, and disagreements about what it meant to be the people of God after the Exile. For some, as we will see, the language of revenge, violence, and regaining power became uppermost in their minds. These voices are definitely part of the biblical record. But there are other voices in the debate, too, and any serious discussion of biblical history must insist that both kinds of voices be heard.

Finally, however, later in the exilic period, a singular prophet makes his (or her) mark—a prophet whose name we do not even know, but a prophet who has made some of the most strikingly original contributions to biblical theology in the entire biblical text. This is a prophet who would have such an influence on the later development of Christian thought that it is hard to exaggerate the importance of the prophet we call "Second Isaiah" (or "Deutero-Isaiah"). This is the prophet whose speeches or writings appear in the book of Isaiah, but starting only with chapter 40. Scholars have long understood that whoever wrote chapters 40–66, the writer(s) were certainly much later than Isaiah of Jerusalem, the prophet we hear about in the first thirty-nine chapters. Furthermore, this later prophet's *influence* is perhaps best summarized in the work of a powerful parable we call the book of Jonah. A full discussion of this, however, is a matter of the chapters that follow. Let us now briefly summarize the importance of the **second** destruction of the Temple as the setting for the final composition of the Gospels of Jesus Christ.

THE SECOND CRITICAL EVENT: THE JEWISH REVOLT OF 66–70 CE

After the Babylonian Exile, there was no serious political or military attempt to regain power as an independent Jewish nation until the centuries just before the time of Jesus. Some of the Hebrew people were able to achieve brief and temporary military power in the revolts that started about 165 years before Jesus. The history of these revolts is outlined in the books of Maccabees, which is why these books are such important historical sources. The times remained volatile and unstable, however, right through the period of the life of Jesus and came to an explosive conclusion just after the death and resurrection of Jesus.

There was one more major, and ill-fated, attempt to reestablish independent rule that occurred some forty years *after* the death and resurrection of Jesus. It occurred precisely in the earliest "New Testament" period when the Gospels were being formulated, in the time when early Christianity was just beginning. This was the Jewish Revolt of 66–70 CE. In order to understand the significance of this violent attempt to revolt against Roman authority in Palestine, however, we need to review the impact of Roman rule in Palestine, which began with Pompey's arrival in Palestine before the time of Jesus (circa 64 BCE).

In recent New Testament scholarship, many scholars have contributed important work that helps modern Christian readers of the New Testament to remember that the violence of the Roman conquest of Palestine is a critically necessary background to any serious understanding of the teachings of Jesus, just as much as it is crucial to read much of the Old Testament in the light of the many crises created by the Babylonian Exile.[8]

The situation of Roman Palestine was, if anything, even more complex than the period of the Greek rulers before the Romans arrived. By the time of the Roman control of this region, for example, the Jewish peoples had divided up into rival religious and political factions. It is important to remember that there was no single way of being a Jew in the centuries before and during the early Christian movement. The book of Maccabees, which recounts the wars between certain Jewish groups and the occupying Greek forces after Alexander the Great's conquests in 333, mentions not only conflicts with foreign Greek soldiers but also conflicts between Jews who did not agree with the Maccabean attitude of hostility toward the Greek rulers, nor did they all agree about influences of Greek culture. The wars described in many of the Jewish sources were, therefore, often as much "civil wars" as "nationalist" wars of independence. In fact, to read them as "wars of independence" is to take a side in those wars against those Jews who favored Greek culture and Greek ways of thinking—even if only moderately. (The Wisdom of Solomon, for example, is clearly from a Jewish writer who knew Platonic thought very well.) These rival factions, often violent toward each other, continued to be a problem for the Roman rulers over Palestine as well.

Part of the setting of the first century when Jesus lived, of course, is Roman political and economic ambitions. The Roman

Empire was aggressive in its goals to rule the world. In the comments that follow, I am especially indebted to Klaus Wengst's important work *Pax Romana and the Peace of Jesus Christ*.

The Roman historian Plutarch describes the Roman general's destruction on the frontiers in what is today Germany: "For fifty miles around he wasted the country with sword and flame. Neither age nor sex inspired pity: places sacred and profane were razed indifferently to the ground."[9]

Another Roman historian, Tacitus, cites (or creates?) a speech from a defeated leader of the native British peoples who resisted Rome, who describes Roman desires as follows:

> If their enemy has wealth, they have greed; if he is poor, they are ambitious; East and West have glutted them.... To plunder, butcher, steal, these things they misname empire; they make a desolation and call it peace. Children and kin are by the law of nature each man's dearest possessions: they are swept away from us by conscription to be slaves in other lands; our wives and sisters, even when they escape a soldier's lust, are debauched by self-styled friends and guests; our goods and chattel go for tribute.[10]

Another reality of Roman rule was forced labor. Again, citing the Roman rule over Britain, Tacitus quotes his early "British" leader to say: "Our life and limbs will be used up in building roads through forests and swamps to the accompaniment of gibes and blows." Part of the famous Roman accomplishments in architecture, of course, was the construction of impressive buildings and structures to commemorate their own achievements and to solidify their own rule. New Testament scholar Bruce Malina writes that "Roman architectural structures serve as monuments to the destruction of an old system of social and political control rather than as genuine symbols of a viable new order."[11] In this regard, note the following rabbinic conversation from the time of Roman rule:

> Rabbi Jehuda and Rabbi Simon are conversing. Rabbi Jehuda is amazed at the Roman achievements: "How fine are the works of this people. They have made streets, they have built bridges, they

have erected baths." Simon answers him: "All what they have made they made to themselves, they built market places, to set harlots in them; baths, to rejuvienate themselves, bridges, to levy tolls for them."[12]

There was a great deal of variation in the kinds of violence imposed on occupied Palestine, but New Testament scholar Marcus Borg mentions exorbitant fines and taxes which could amount to a large percent of a person's income.[13] In fact, he writes, the introduction of Roman rule brought "a crisis in all aspects of Jewish life."[14] Other scholars report that throughout the empire, especially in the time of Nero (54–68 CE), anyone who was in debt over tax payments to the ruling authorities was liable to slavery.[15] New Testament historian Richard Horsley notes that Herod increased the already oppressive taxation to support his regime and his lavish building projects.[16]

Knowing all of this lends further meaning to an interesting passage written by the Jewish historian Josephus. He described the standard equipment of Roman soldiers: each soldier carried a spear and a long shield, saw and basket, spade and axe, and thong of leather and a hook and handcuffs. Klaus Wengst's commentary on this list is illuminating:

> First come the weapons which are used for the conquest of foreign territory. The implements listed after this certainly also had a military purpose, in that they were used for digging trenches and building camps, but they also served for the economic exploitation of conquered territory. The handcuffs at the end stand for the maintenance of the new situation brought about by force of arms.[17]

Finally, Roman occupation often meant religious pressures as well as exclusively or mainly economic pressures as well. But was it better for Jews or Christians outside of the trouble spot of Palestine with its frequent outbursts of violence against Roman occupation?

In fact, simply being a Jew or Christian outside of Judean territories would not necessarily spare you from pressures as well. Christianity, of course, attracted converts from non-Jewish background, and for these converts, there were even more religious and economic pressures to conform to Roman life and expectations. There is certainly evidence for some Roman abuse of Christians during the latter part of the reign of Nero (54–68 CE) and again during the reign of Domitian (81–96 CE).

Christian converts, especially in Asia Minor, today the area of Turkey, faced the pressures of the Imperial Roman religious cults and the resulting possibility of persecution for refusing to participate in this form of state religion. It has recently been noted, for example, that the seven cities addressed in Revelation were all located in Asia Minor, which was under a different governmental status than Judea, which was directly ruled by occupation soldiers from Rome.[18] In Asia Minor, there was less resistance to Roman rule, and the elite in the cities addressed by John were apparently doing reasonably well economically. What is also essential to know, however, is that six of these seven cities addressed in Revelation were centers of the Imperial Cult. We are learning more and more about the nature of the Roman Imperial Cult, that is, the religion established by the empire to encourage religious obedience to the leadership of the empire and a religion that tries to establish a devotion to the empire as "eternal." There is both textual and archaeological evidence mounting up about this widespread Roman creation of a religion of the State. In ceremonies of mass devotion to Roman culture and the symbols of the state, the empire built shrines to living Caesars, and openly encouraged the association of Roman leaders (and their families) with the ancient gods and goddesses of Greece and Rome. Festivals were frequent, involving prayers, sacrifices, and feasting—all centered around "citizenship" and devotion. In short, this was a quasi-religious series of feasts and festivals, with priestly personnel, and all dedicated to honoring the past and present Caesars and generally (and literally) singing the praises of the Roman system. We would call it religious patriotism today, and the cult was particularly active in the cities addressed by John's book of Revelation. John's frequent references to the "Beast," then, were a particularly effective way for the writer to portray the Roman system.

There are spectacular Roman ruins in some of these cities mentioned in the book of Revelation, providing critically important visual backgrounds to this discussion of the significance of Roman rule over Asia Minor. Ephesus, the greatest city of the Roman province of Asia and the seat of the proconsul, also featured an imperial temple and an altar and housed imperial priests to officiate over the Roman cult. In Smyrna, a prosperous port city, there was also a temple, an altar, and a priesthood. Pergamum, the capital of Asia, was a center of imperial worship for the entire region featuring a great acropolis, an altar to Zeus, and a temple to Augustus. Thyatira, famous for traders and artisans, also featured imperial religious ruins. Sardis, regional capital of Sudia in Asia Minor, Philadelphia, and Laodicea (the richest city in Phrygia, known for banks and linen and cotton, and also medical school and pharmacies)—all were equally active centers of the Roman religious cult. Part of the force of the book of Revelation, then, may well be an attempt to discourage Christians from participation in the imperial cults by contrasting true devotion to Jesus with false devotion to the state religion of the Caesars as gods.

So, in the light of political, economic, and religious oppression under Roman occupation—the New Testament asks, "How do we understand the call to be God's people in the shadows of the *second* destruction of the Temple?" Some Jews, of course, called for violent resistance. The various factions and groups that engaged in violent resistance to Roman occupation have been well documented by many New Testament scholars and need not detain us here. Suffice it to say that the resistance was active and constant, offering always the possibility to be involved in anti-Roman violence. The resistance grew to fever pitch with the Jewish war between 67–70 CE, culminating in the Roman destruction of Jerusalem and its Temple, and the final defeat of the Jewish resistance at Masada, the hilltop fortress built by Herod.

In this context, New Testament scholar Richard Horsley argues that Jesus called for a new unity among the devastated Jewish people of Palestine and especially directed his message to those disenfranchised Jews—the poor and the neglected—who were suffering the most from Roman occupation and imposition of material and legal structures on the occupied Jewish populations.[19]

More controversial, however, is the suggestion that Jesus' instruction to "Love your enemies" was in reality a call to Jewish solidarity in the face of Roman persecution—it was, therefore, a call only to "us"—and it is a call that does not involve "them"—the Romans or other foreigners. In response to this idea, I would point out that Jesus consistently called for radical "border violations," violating traditional and normal definitions of "the people of God." Jesus openly included many controversial persons of the Palestinian society of his era, including repentant centurions, Canaanite women, Samaritans, as well as Jews from various factions. In fact, it is precisely Jesus' own "border running" that established an important tradition among early Christians—flouting human borders for the sake of the gospel.

The Christian Bible constructs an image of Jesus as a violator of borders, just as Jonah (and other minority Hebrew coyotes) violated borders. One of the most impressive borders that Jonah and Jesus both violated was the border between the violent "us" and the violent "them." In other words, both biblical figures violated the most violent borders constructed in their times: the borders of warring enemies. More about this in the following chapters.

FIRST-CENTURY DEBATES ABOUT VIOLENCE: A CASE STUDY

We noted that, in response to the older exilic events, conflicts broke out between community members about which way the people of God should go. One might put it this way: the debate was either "renationalize" or "redefine." Jeremiah even drew the conclusion that God wanted the exilic community to refrain from violent revolt, and "seek the peace of the city" where God sent them (Jeremiah 29). Before we leave the New Testament background, I want to point out that Jesus and Paul, among others, were not the only Jews who questioned the violence of their age. There were non-Christian Jewish leaders who questioned the revolt against Rome as well. The point is that just as there was an "Old Testament" debate between different paths on the question of what it meant to be "the people of God" after the Exile of 587 BCE, so there was a debate in the first century among Jews under Roman occupation as well. We know that two Jews especially— namely Jesus (Matthew 5–6) and Paul (Romans 12)—took strong positions against violence. Their teaching came before the Jewish Revolt of 66–70, and the evidence shows that the Christians, while suffering from the Roman destruction of Jerusalem at the end of that revolt, did not participate in the revolt itself. Were there any other Jews, perhaps among those not associated with the Christian movement, who questioned the violence of the revolt as well? Some Christians may be surprised to find out that some Pharisees also deeply questioned violence.

Jesus is often portrayed as arguing with Pharisees, and as a result, many Christians have developed the mistaken notion that the Pharisees were particularly bad Jewish leaders. This is not really accurate. Paul was himself a convert from Pharisees, and there appears to have been many Pharisees who joined Jesus as followers, yet maintained their Pharisaic Jewish commitments and perspectives as well. While it seems beyond question that Jesus had serious disagreements with some of the Pharisees that he had contact with, there are other Pharasaic leaders of the first century who have views very similar to the teachings of Jesus and the early Christians.

In fact, there was at least one major issue upon which many Pharisees seemed to agree with Jesus and the early Christians, even those Pharisees who did not follow Jesus or become part of his movement. A great deal of the Pharisees' response to the violence of Palestine was a nonmilitant opposition to the Jewish revolutionaries who sought to violently overthrow Roman rule. This is not because these Jewish leaders thought favorably about Roman rule (they most certainly did not), but rather they thought that resistance to Roman oppression must not be violent. In the case of some non-Christian Jewish leaders, this is best illustrated by citing the teachings and traditions attributed to the first-century Pharisaic leader Rabbi Yohanan ben Zakkai, who was an elder Jewish leader by the time of the revolt in 66–70 CE.

It is often suggested that Rabbi Yohanan ben Zakkai inherited his famous opposition to violence from his teacher, Rabbi Hillel, considered one of the great founders of the rabbinic traditions that are the textual building blocks of modern Judaism. According to the Jewish scholar Jacob Neusner, "It would have been from Hillel that Yohanan ben Zakkai acquired his dedication to the ideal of peace, for Hillel had said, 'Be of the disciples of Aaron, living peace and pursuing peace, loving mankind and drawing all men to Torah.' From Hillel, Yohanan would have learned, second, that the sage has the responsibility to concern himself with pressing social problems."[20]

In a story recounted in more than one ancient source, Rabbi Yohanan ben Zakkai opposed the Jewish Revolt against Rome while a resident in Jerusalem. The rabbi had his followers fool the Jewish revolutionary guards at the gates of Jerusalem so that he could escape with his disciples. He did this, according to Josephus, by placing himself in a coffin and having his followers carry him out "to be buried." Once outside the city, he had a conversation with the Roman leaders and worked out a separate peace whereby the rabbi could move to a coastal town, Yavneh, and establish a school of Jewish learning. How important was Rabbi Yohanan ben Zakkai's defiant act of nonviolence? Many modern Jewish scholars credit Rabbi Yohanan ben Zakkai's opposition to the Jewish Revolt and his establishment of his Academy in Yavneh as quite simply one of the main ways that Judaism survived the first century.

A second famous passage attributed to Rabbi Yohanan ben Zakkai in Rabbinic literature reflects his peaceful teachings. Consider the following rabbinic discussion that begins with a reflection on Exodus 20:25, the passage that forbids sacrificial altars being made of stones that have been hewn, that is, stones that have come into contact with metal. One famous rabbinic interpretation of this passage is that swords are made from metal, and swords end life. Altars, on the other hand, prolong life by seeking forgiveness from God for sins. So, something that ends life should not come into contact with something that grants life. What is particularly striking is the extended discussion attributed to Rabbi Yohanan ben Zakkai, who calls these stones that make an altar "stones that establish peace," and then continues with the interesting suggestion that *persons can become the "stones of the altar"* with whom iron weapons should not come in contact. It is worth reading the ancient passage in which the rabbi teaches his lesson:

> The stones for the altar do not see nor hear nor speak. Yet because they serve to establish peace between Israel and their Father in heaven, the Holy One, blessed be He, said, You shall lift up no iron tool upon them (Deut. 27:5). How much the more then should he who establishes peace between man and his fellow-man, between husband and wife, between city and city, between nation and nation, between family and family, between government and government, be protected so that no harm should come to him.[21]

Many Jewish scholars have noted the significant ethos of peacefulness that was characteristic of some strands of first-century rabbinic teaching, as recounted in later rabbinic texts. A famous rabbinic passage quotes a number of rabbis expressing their aversion to killing by stating: "Had we been members of the Sanhedrin when it had the power of capital punishment, no man would ever have been executed by it."[22] Josephus commented that "Pharisees are naturally lenient in the matter of punishments" (Ant. 17:288-98). Finally, in a tradition that is strikingly reminiscent of the case of Jesus and the woman caught committing adultery in John 8, Rabbi Yohanan ben Zakkai questioned the mandatory eyewitnesses of a capital case. When the supposed witnesses could not answer the detailed questions put to them by the rabbi, the capital punishment was commuted. It is clear from the context that it was the rabbi's every intention to prevent the execution—in keeping with the same "anti-killing" ethos reflected in other sources. It is arguable that Jesus discredited any valid witnesses in very much the same manner—by questioning whether anyone present was a valid witness (i.e., "without sin").

As for the reputation of Rabbi Yohanan ben Zakkai as a teacher of peace, an important modern Jewish historian has observed that Rabbi Yohanan ben Zakkai taught that even the Romans can be forgiven their destructions if they repent. Hanina, a priest colleague of his, said, "He not only taught that 'great is peace, for it is the equivalent of all the works of creation,' but also taking a cue from Jeremiah, explained 'You shall pray for the welfare of the kingdom.' "[23]

Finally, and related to this, is the wonderful tradition of Rabbi Yohanan ben Zakkai teaching about the importance of justice:

> Once as Rabban Yohanan ben Zakkai was coming out of Jerusalem, Rabbi Joshua followed after him, and beheld the Temple in ruins. Woe unto us, Rabbi Joshua cried, that this place, the place where the iniquities of Israel were atoned for is laid waste. My son, Rabban Yohanan said to him, be not grieved. We have another atonement as effective as this, and what is it? It is acts of loving-kindness, as it is said, "For I desire mercy and not sacrifice" (Hosea 6:6).[24]

CONCLUSION

These samples are sufficient to establish that there was a strain of antimilitarist peacefulness, and perhaps full-blown nonviolence, in some first-century rabbinic thought, and that this peaceful ethic tends to focus around the traditions of Rabbi Yohanan ben Zakkai and his opposition to the war against Roman-occupying armies. Of course, his views engendered opposition, and his anti-war ethos has been argued, and continues to be debated, by Jewish scholars to this day.[25]

The point is simply this—the first century is both deeply distressing as a time of great violence, and at the same time, strikingly creative as a time of consideration of different paths forward. It is in this context that Jesus sets forth his radical program of violating borders and widens the meaning of "Love your enemies" to include even the enemy other, the minority other, and the female other. It is to these voices of the border violators, in both the Old Testament and New Testament, that we now turn.

Chapter Three

"Second Isaiah" and Jonah: Two Hebrew Coyotes ...

We have examined the context of the Babylonian Exile and the Jewish Revolt against the Romans a generation after the time of Jesus, and now we understand the fearsome destruction and the forced reformulation of identity that arises from this kind of conquest. People in these circumstances must face resettlement and refugee status in the modern world as well as in biblical history. Now we take the time to ask: what impact did these events have on religious and social thinking about what it means to be the "people of God"? Let us begin with the Babylonian Exile in the Old Testament.

We need to begin by examining two different perspectives in response to Exile. There are more than merely two—and they are more complex—but let us examine two streams or traditions of thought. On the one hand, one can see the quest for vengeance and power over one's enemies (probably the majority view). On the other hand, however, one can just as clearly see the desire for transformation and coexistence. These latter, perhaps minority, voices represent the Hebrew coyotes crossing borders. Let us start, however, with the more familiar view represented in those passages in the Bible that responded to the Exile by calling for vengeance on Babylon, in these paraphrased words from Psalm 137, "Happy are those who pay you back."

Vengeance and Power over Enemies

It is entirely understandable that one of the most powerful responses to the exile is unmitigated anger: "Babylon must be punished." Psalm 137 (the initial section of which is often read in churches and synagogues) offers a glimpse into the Israelites' sheer outrage at their conquest and forced resettlement:

> **Psalm 137:1-9:** By the rivers of Babylon—there we sat down and there we wept when we remembered Zion. On the willows there we hung up our harps. For there our captors asked us for songs, and our tormentors asked for mirth, saying, "Sing us one of the songs of Zion." How could we sing the LORD's song in a foreign land? If I forget you, O Jerusalem, let my right hand wither. Let my tongue cling to the roof of my mouth, if I do not remember you, if I do not set Jerusalem above my highest joy. Remember, O LORD, against the Edomites the day of Jerusalem's fall, how they said, "Tear it down. Tear it down. Down to its foundations." O daughter Babylon, you devastator. Happy shall they be who pay you back what you have done to us. Happy shall they be who take your little ones and dash them against the rock.

Other psalms written after the Exile include similar themes of punishment:

> **Psalm 149:4-9:** For the LORD takes pleasure in his people; he adorns the humble with victory. Let the faithful exult in glory; let them sing for joy on their couches. Let the high praises of God be in their throats and two-edged swords in their hands, to execute vengeance on the nations and punishment on the peoples, to bind their kings with fetters and their nobles with chains of iron, to execute on them the judgment decreed. This is glory for all his faithful ones. Praise the LORD.

I think any honest reader of the Bible can confess that they have felt this kind of anger and desire for "payback." How we read such expressions of anger in the Bible will be the subject of chapter 8, but for now there is an interesting question to ask about these angry passages: if the book of Deuteronomy warned that the Exile would be the result of Israel's sin (Deuteronomy 28), and Jeremiah repeated this, why would the nations like Babylon be punished for being the tool of God? Because, teach some of the prophets, they went too far. The punishment was too great, too cruel, and they never paid the price for this cruelty.

For example, Zechariah, writing some seventy years after the destruction of Jerusalem by Nebuchadnezzar and even after the Persian conquest of Babylon by Cyrus the Great, speaks about the "four horsemen" who run errands for God. The four horsemen are images that return in later apocalyptic writing like Revelation, but in Zechariah they are heavenly messengers who ride throughout the earth only to discover that the earth is *too* peaceful, *too* comfortable, despite the fact that the Israelites still suffer the results of their exile. The prophet writes that God is angry with the comforts of the world while Hebrews still suffer:

> **Zechariah 1:15-16:** I am extremely *angry* with the nations that are at ease; for while I was only a *little angry*, they made the disaster worse. Therefore, thus says the LORD, I have returned to Jerusalem with compassion; my house shall be built in it, says the LORD of hosts, and the measuring line shall be stretched out over Jerusalem.

For many biblical writers, God's return, and also the people's return to the land, will mean punishing violence against foreign rulers and foreign nations. At the end of Jeremiah, Babylon herself is threatened with great disasters, her primary gods will be humiliated:

> **Jeremiah 50:2b-15:** Her images are put to shame, her idols are dismayed. For out of the north a nation has come up against her; it shall make her land a desolation, and no one shall live in it; both human beings and animals shall flee away.

The images used in this same chapter of Jeremiah may well have later inspired the story in the book of Daniel (Daniel 4) where there is a dream of God "cutting the tree" (representing the Babylonian Empire) and releasing the captive "animals" under it. Here, Jeremiah commands that people should be "like goats" and flee from Babylon to escape its impending doom:

> **Jeremiah 50:8-10:** Flee from Babylon, and go out of the land of the Chaldeans, and be like male goats leading the flock. For I am going to stir up and bring against Babylon a company of great nations from the land of the north; and they shall array themselves against her; from there she shall be taken. Their arrows are like the arrows of a skilled warrior who does not return empty-handed. Chaldea shall be plundered; all who plunder her shall be sated, says the LORD.

Finally, in a scene that is reminiscent of the fall of Jericho, Babylon will be destroyed like the other devastating foreign power of Assyria, which was destroyed before the time of Babylon:

> **Jeremiah 50:14-18:** Take up your positions around Babylon, all you that bend the bow; shoot at her, spare no arrows, for she has sinned against the LORD. Raise a shout against her from all sides, "She has surrendered; her bulwarks have fallen, her walls are thrown down." For this is the vengeance of the LORD: take vengeance on her, do to her as she has done. Cut off from Babylon the sower, and the wielder of the sickle in time of harvest; because of the destroying sword all of them shall return to their own people, and all of them shall flee to their own land. Israel is a hunted sheep driven away by lions. First the king of Assyria devoured it, and now at the end King Nebuchadrezzar of Babylon has gnawed its bones. Therefore, thus says the LORD of hosts, the God of Israel: I am going to punish the king of Babylon and his land, as I punished the king of Assyria.

This angry expectation of punishment extends to those nations, like Edom, who are accused of assisting the Babylonians when Jerusalem fell. In fact, the entire little book of Obadiah is a long, angry single chapter aimed against Edom, and only Edom, for its participation in the destruction of Jerusalem: "I will surely make you least among the nations; you shall be utterly despised" (v. 2). Drawing on the old story that Edom is descended from

Esau, the brother of Jacob, the prophet seems especially angry at what seemed like betrayal:

> **Obadiah 1:10-13:** For the slaughter and violence done to your brother Jacob, shame shall cover you, and you shall be cut off forever. On the day that you stood aside, on the day that strangers carried off his wealth, and foreigners entered his gates and cast lots for Jerusalem, you too were like one of them. But you should not have gloated over your brother on the day of his misfortune; you should not have rejoiced over the people of Judah on the day of their ruin; you should not have boasted on the day of distress.

What will this punishment mean for the people of God? For many visionaries, it will mean a return to Israelite power—even an empire—before which the nations will bow low, in a subservient role as mere servants or slaves. This is a theme probably drawn from older royal sayings about the power of the king over Jerusalem. In an older Psalm from the time of the monarchy, we read about this proposed dominion of the Hebrew king over many nations:

> **Psalm 72:8-11:** May he have dominion from sea to sea, and from the River to the ends of the earth. May his foes bow down before him, and his enemies lick the dust. May the kings of Tarshish and of the isles render him tribute, may the kings of Sheba and Seba bring gifts. May all kings fall down before him, all nations give him service.

So, this theme of the nations "licking the dust" is revived in passages after the Exile, as a theme of punishment for the nations who were so violent. This suggests restoring older promises of vengeance and restored power over the nations:

> **Isaiah 49:23:** Kings shall be your foster fathers, and their queens your nursing mothers. With their faces to the ground they shall bow down to you, and lick the dust of your feet. Then you will know that I am the LORD; those who wait for me shall not be put to shame.

Like other empires, this new Israelite empire will also exploit the resources of others:

Isaiah 60:11-12: Your gates shall always be open; day and night they shall not be shut, so that nations shall bring you their wealth, with their kings led in procession. For the nation and kingdom that will not serve you shall perish; those nations shall be utterly laid waste.

Such visions are frightening. I think it is important, however, that we hear these expressions as normal human responses to devastation. I believe that people have a right to be angry over injustice. But eventually, we need to reflect on what to do in response to such anger-making situations.

We have to ask: are these visions of dominance and power representative of the ancient Hebrews at their most impressive moments of faith? I don't think so. We must confess, however, to its familiarity. I hate to admit it, but I certainly recognize these feelings of anger, and I confess to a temptation for revenge in the wake of something I find unfair or unjust before I sense the genuine spirit of Christ leading me to calm down and assess all the issues with his values in mind, and not simply my hurt feelings. Jesus himself was tempted by a promise of the nations being given over to him (Matt. 4:8), and perhaps we should understand that the temptation involved these nations "bowing down" to Jesus in language familiar to the revenge language of some parts of the Old Testament and the forced submission of the nations.

Do I believe that the writers of these Old Testament passages themselves deeply believed that this vengeance was what God was promising them? How can I deny it, when I not only know what this feels like myself but also when I hear faithful people around the world insist that God promises them precisely these kinds of vengeful acts and world dominion? Of course, people confuse the command of God with the angry desire for revenge. But are moments of anger the only true ones? Proverbs 14:29 suggests that being "slow to anger" reveals that one has great understanding. Maybe we should use these wise words to read the Bible more carefully?

Anger can twist words into something destructive. Modern readers of the Bible can even take positive biblical ideas and angrily turn them into shameful and negative ideas. For example, consider the ancient Christian hymn from the Epistle to the Philippians that proclaims, "at the name of Jesus every knee should bend, in heaven and on earth and under the earth, and every tongue should confess that Jesus Christ is Lord, to the glory of God the Father." As a statement that many people will come to recognize the love of God, this is a wonderful sentiment that hopes for the best for all people. But this same idea can start to sound angry and vengeful—as if God will **force** everyone to bend his or her knee. Such talk can be dangerous if we see ourselves as the agents of this forced submission to the name of Jesus—if we think that by our military power or overwhelming authority we can bring about the promise's fulfillment.

I acknowledge the angry tradition in the Hebrew scriptures. It is there—it cannot be avoided. There were many who passionately believed that the promise of vengeance and restored power was God's promised path forward for the people of God. They believed that they should reestablish borders and reestablish power to police those borders. But the presence of this attitude only serves to highlight the reality of its alternative—those Old Testament coyotes who at the same time ran those boundaries and questioned those conceptions of the path God's people should take.

TRANSFORMATIONS OF THE ENEMY

An entirely different spirit can be heard in other biblical texts that also speak of the relationship to the nations. We can cite passages often considered to be post-exilic (but which might be earlier) such as Micah; passages that suggest some different ways of thinking. Here, we begin to see that the desire for punishment is mitigated now with a sense that many may come to understand the evil of their behavior and actually feel shame:

Micah 7:15-17: As in the days when you came out of the land of Egypt, show us marvelous things. The nations shall see and be ashamed of all their might; they shall lay their hands on their mouths; their ears shall be deaf; they shall lick dust like a snake, like the crawling things of the earth; they shall come trembling out of their fortresses; they shall turn in dread to the LORD our God, and they shall stand in fear of you.

Notice the difference between being forced and making choices for themselves—the difference is between conquest and confession. It is quite proper to insist that this difference must be recognized so that all such passages are not lumped together as speaking with one voice.

Perhaps the most famous Hebrew "coyote" and border runner of them all, however, is the voice we often call "Second Isaiah" (Deutero-Isaiah)—an unnamed prophet (or at the very least, a radically inspired editor) who introduced some other thoughts to the older text of Isaiah the Prophet. Who exactly was Second Isaiah? We are likely to never know.

Biblical scholars and readers have been quite certain for over a century now that the parts of Isaiah we call chapters 40–55 (and many include 56–66) were written long after the time of Isaiah the Prophet, who lived in the late eighth century BCE, during the Assyrian Empire. The reason that these writings were added to the writings of Isaiah the Prophet (chapters 1–39) is probably because this prophet we call "Second Isaiah" was a follower, a "disciple" (more probably a disciple of a disciple) of the original prophet. This would explain such famous problems as Isaiah 1 introducing the prophet as having started his ministry "in the days of King Uzziah" (who died in 740 BCE) and yet Isaiah 45:1 specifically mentioning Cyrus the Persian ruler who conquered Babylon in 539. In other words, some parts are later.

Furthermore, there is an interesting opinion, held by a small minority of scholars, that this Deutero-Isaiah may also have been a female prophet (Isa. 8:3). There is certainly no inherent reason why not—after all, Isaiah himself was married to a prophet, and women certainly were prophets throughout Israelite history (Exod. 15:20; Judg. 4:4; 2 Kings 24:14; Neh. 6:14). Some have wondered: in the call for compassion so powerful in Isaiah 40–55, do we hear a female critique of largely male violence? Whatever we may know, or not know, about this prophet, I believe that it is hard to exaggerate the impact of the thought of Second Isaiah and this prophet's keen insights into the will of God for a transformed future for the Israelite people.

Second Isaiah begins with a dynamic call that times have changed:

> **Isaiah 40:1-5:** Comfort, O comfort my people, says your God. Speak tenderly to Jerusalem, and cry to her that she has served her term, that her penalty is paid, that she has received from the LORD's hand double for all her sins. A voice cries out: "In the wilderness prepare the way of the LORD, make straight in the desert a highway for our God. Every valley shall be lifted up, and every mountain and hill be made low; the uneven ground shall become level, and the rough places a plain. Then the glory of the LORD shall be revealed, and all people shall see it together, for the mouth of the LORD has spoken."

Preparing a "way in the wilderness" and a "highway in the desert" are echoes of the Exodus deliverance from Egypt generations before. What this prophet proclaims is a "new exodus"— God will soon lead the people away from Babylon just as God led the slaves from Egypt. But why is this coming now? Two things are interesting to note: first the idea that Jerusalem has "served her term," and the other that someone is coming "from the East." First, remember that Jeremiah had proclaimed that the Exile was the direct result of the sins of the people. So, this word is a direct response to that older biblical theology that guided not only Jeremiah but also the historical books like 1–2 Kings as well. Now, it is as if the unnamed prophet is saying, "Yes, that was true, but now we have served the term of punishment, it is a new day." The second development, however, is the approach of someone very important:

> **Isaiah 41:2-4:** Who has roused a victor from the east, summoned him to his service? He delivers up nations to him, and tramples kings under foot; he makes them like dust with his sword, like

driven stubble with his bow. He pursues them and passes on safely,
scarcely touching the path with his feet. Who has performed and
done this, calling the generations from the beginning? I, the LORD,
am first, and will be with the last.

This one coming from the "east" is thus named explicitly later
in the book:

Isaiah 45:1-4: Thus says the LORD to his anointed, to Cyrus, whose
right hand I have grasped to subdue nations before him and strip
kings of their robes, to open doors before him—and the gates shall
not be closed: I will go before you and level the mountains, I will
break in pieces the doors of bronze and cut through the bars of
iron, I will give you the treasures of darkness and riches hidden in
secret places, so that you may know that it is I, the LORD, the God
of Israel, who call you by your name. For the sake of my servant
Jacob, and Israel my chosen, I call you by your name, I surname
you, though you do not know me.

So, given that a major change is coming—it is a time to reflect
on what this experience has meant—what are the new things that
God may be doing with God's people. Second Isaiah refers to the
exiled community as God's "servant":

Isaiah 41:8-10: But you, Israel, my servant, Jacob, whom I have
chosen, the offspring of Abraham, my friend; you whom I took
from the ends of the earth, and called from its farthest corners,
saying to you, "You are my servant, I have chosen you and not
cast you off"; do not fear, for I am with you, do not be afraid, for I
am your God; I will strengthen you, I will help you, I will uphold
you with my victorious right hand.

But what is the role of the suffering of this servant? What has
been accomplished by the Babylonian Exile? For Second Isaiah,
part of the answer involves a transformed relationship to "the
nations." It is here that this prophet delivers a shocking word—
and with that word *dashes across a major border* in the minds of the
people. There are, apparently, new plans for the old enemies:

Isaiah 49:6-7: He says, "It is too light a thing that you should be my servant to raise up the tribes of Jacob and to restore the survivors of Israel; I will give you as a light to the nations, that my salvation may reach to the end of the earth." Thus says the LORD, the Redeemer of Israel and his Holy One, to one deeply despised, abhorred by the nations, the slave of rulers, "Kings shall see and stand up, princes, and they shall prostrate themselves, because of the LORD, who is faithful, the Holy One of Israel, who has chosen you."

The idea that "the nations" will share in God's plans for a new age of humanity is one of the most dynamic concepts of Second Isaiah. It is clear that the light to the nations leads directly to "kings and princes" who will react in confession and repentance. That, at least, is the interesting hope being suggested here. When I am asked, as I am on occasion, if I believe that God really "inspired" scripture, I often go to this passage and say something like: "How could any person think this way without the Spirit of God moving them?" I confess that I am deeply moved by the fact that a prophet from amongst a people who have suffered such a traumatic series of events has lifted his (or her) eyes to see that their suffering will be transformed toward a startling goal— the salvation of **all** the nations. Instead of vengeance, salvation. Instead of destruction, peace.

One of the most important Native American writers in America in the twentieth century was surely the late Dr. Vine Deloria. He was a severe (but, sadly, usually quite accurate) critic of Christian behavior toward American Indians. In one article, however, he wrote that Native Americans, out of their suffering, may well come to understand profound religious truths that they will then be able to share with the rest of humanity.[1] Similarly, when an Armenian or Jewish teacher calls for an end to *all* violence, they speak with an authority that comes from profound suffering. I believe this comes from God. Humans are typically capable only of revenge, or even more typically thinking that their own violence is pure and innocent while the enemies' violence is bad and evil. Second Isaiah, however, proposes that God calls us to now be "a light to the nations," and not only a source of recovery for ourselves.

Let us be very careful about this idea of the future of "the nations." Note that the nations appear to repent—we are not talking about ignoring injustice. We are speaking about a genuine vision of reconciliation not unlike the spirit of the "Truth and Reconciliation" movements in South Africa and often proposed for Ireland. As we have clearly shown, it seems that we have a very emotional debate within the scripture on how this relationship with "the nations" is going to go. On the one hand, Second Isaiah's idea about being a "light to the nations" inspires some profound hopes about a day without war and violence. Most scholars believe, for example, that one of the most famous peace passages in the entire Bible was actually inspired by Second Isaiah and "edited in" to the place it now occupies in both Isaiah and Micah, two prophets who actually lived decades before the time of Second Isaiah.

> **Isaiah 2:4-5:** He shall judge between the nations, and shall arbitrate for many peoples; they shall beat their swords into plowshares, and their spears into pruning hooks; nation shall not lift up sword against nation, neither shall they learn war any more. O house of Jacob, come, let us walk in the light of the LORD.

It has been my experience, however, that no sooner does one cite this passage, than one hears sneering references back to the more violent passages. They quite rightly point out that there are other passages that represent this procession of the nations to Zion as resulting from violent judgment and threat. And, I acknowledge that there are passages that strongly suggest this. Some passages suggest that the march to Zion is a forced march of the conquered. What must also be acknowledged but rarely is, however, is the fact that the *other, more peaceful view also does exist* in scripture as well—the view that holds out great hope for the transformation of the enemy.

It cannot be avoided that there is a debate in the biblical books—a disagreement as to how God is leading God's people—

with regard to our relationships with "the nations." It is important to insist that the reconciling side of the debate be represented and heard. The violent passages must not be allowed to overrule the Hebrew voices for peace and reconciliation. Again, violence must not be allowed to trump peace—especially by the ill-chosen criterion that "majority rules." Jesus, too, was the leader of a minority opinion, after all. These are the voices of the coyotes—the border runners—that are typically silenced in the shouting in the churches about God as a "God of War." But these peaceful voices are part of scripture too.

As we have argued, however, even those biblical voices who hold to a punishment of the evil of the nations (and justice demands some recognition of that violence and evil that has occurred) hold out the possibility of a resulting transformation. Another passage often considered to be our later "radical editor" inspired by Second Isaiah, is Isaiah 19:20-25. Here, the writer speaks of Egyptians crying out to God and God hearing them. What follows is punishment of the guilty, "striking," but immediately afterward, a healing. And this is finished by one of the most profoundly radical visions of peaceful coexistence in all of scripture—the concluding three-part blessing on the three former arch-enemies:

> **Isaiah 19:20-25:** It will be a sign and a witness to the LORD of hosts in the land of Egypt; when they cry to the LORD because of oppressors, he will send them a savior, and will defend and deliver them. The LORD will make himself known to the Egyptians; and the Egyptians will know the LORD on that day, and will worship with sacrifice and burnt offering, and they will make vows to the LORD and perform them. The LORD will strike Egypt, striking and healing; they will return to the LORD, and he will listen to their supplications and heal them. On that day there will be a highway from Egypt to Assyria, and the Assyrian will come into Egypt, and the Egyptian into Assyria, and the Egyptians will worship with the Assyrians. On that day Israel will be the third with Egypt and Assyria, a blessing in the midst of the earth, whom the LORD of hosts has blessed, saying, "Blessed be Egypt my people, and Assyria the work of my hands, and Israel my heritage."

Other radical writers speak of "the nations" actually choosing to learn about God. Zechariah looks to a day when the Gentiles will recognize their need for God:

> **Zechariah 8:20-23:** Thus says the LORD of hosts: Peoples shall yet come, the inhabitants of many cities; the inhabitants of one city shall go to another, saying, "Come, let us go to entreat the favor of the LORD, and to seek the LORD of hosts; I myself am going." Many peoples and strong nations shall come to seek the LORD of hosts in Jerusalem, and to entreat the favor of the LORD. Thus says the LORD of hosts: In those days ten men from nations of every language shall take hold of a Jew, grasping his garment and saying, "Let us go with you, for we have heard that God is with you."

There is a tendency among some readers of Isaiah (and other passages) to take all positive references to "the nations" to be references to Jews who are living in those nations, not the foreign peoples themselves. Thus, for example, Isaiah 19 is taken to refer to Jews living in the Mesopotamian and Egyptian diaspora, but not the Assyrians and Egyptians themselves. But this notion of being "a light to the nations" most certainly did inspire one Hebrew coyote to think otherwise—and this writer ends up telling the story of the greatest (and ironically, the most reluctant) border runner in the entire Hebrew Bible—Jonah.

JONAH: THE RELUCTANT COYOTE

The most powerful biblical witness to a Hebrew theology of crossing borders is the little book of Jonah, which presents us with some fascinating difficulties, but also some of the most potentially profound ideas in the entire Old Testament. It is unfortunate, although understandable, that the story has often been written off as merely a child's story. I admit that the story of a man praying in the belly of a fish cries out for children's Bible illustrations and good puppet theatre. Just as distracting, however, are the frankly silly attempts to do pseudo-scientific work on just how long a human being could survive in the gullet of a large fish so that one can prove that it is a literal report and not a religious story. In other words, wooden "literalism" is almost as skilled at missing the point as are those who make it just a children's Sunday school lesson. I would strongly argue that Jonah is first and foremost a parable for adults.

It is universally held among biblical scholars working on Jonah that the book is post-587, and thus comes from a late period in the history of the Hebrew people. Therefore, the city of Nineveh, where Jonah is sent to go, is clearly symbolic. (Second Maccabees 13:9 conflates Assyria with Babylon, and these names are used well into the New Testament—note the use of Babylon in 1 Peter 5:13, and in Revelation 18 to refer to the Roman Empire.)

The tale is meant to suggest that Jonah is called to deliver his prophetic message to the massive capital city of "the nations," a city of a nation that is a former and famous enemy. As any reader would understand, any **sane** Hebrew who thought that he was called to the Assyrian empire would book passage with Jonah and take the first boat heading for the mysterious "Tarshish"—a name that one could loosely translate as "the middle of nowhere." Jonah soon realizes that there is no escape from the God of the Hebrews, even if one leaves Palestine (an important message for those living in diaspora, by the way). Even in the sea, the "sea monsters," the "great fish" are subservient to God. The non-Hebrew sailors seem familiar with Jonah's God, and are quite concerned that Jonah's disobedience threatens them. (Later Jewish tradition, incidentally, holds that these sailors later converted to Judaism, being so impressed with God's control of the natural elements.)

It is interesting to note, however, that the heart of the book of Jonah is the poem that appears in chapter 2:

Jonah 2:1-9: I called to the LORD out of my distress, and he answered me; out of the belly of Sheol I cried, and you heard my voice. You cast me into the deep, into the heart of the seas, and the flood surrounded me; all your waves and your billows passed over me. Then I said, "I am driven away from your sight; how shall I look again upon your holy temple?" The waters closed in over me; the deep surrounded me; weeds were wrapped around my head at the roots of the mountains. I went down to the land whose bars closed upon me forever; yet you brought up my life from the Pit, O LORD my God. As my life was ebbing away, I remembered the LORD; and my prayer came to you, into your holy temple. Those who worship vain idols forsake their true loyalty. But I with the voice of thanksgiving will sacrifice to you; what I have vowed I will pay. Deliverance belongs to the LORD.

It is likely that this poem (many call it a "psalm") is much older than the tale of Jonah and that the tale was modeled to fit around the psalm—almost like a story to illustrate the meaning of the psalm (an ancient homily?) or what rabbis called a midrash. Note, for example, some of the important references in the psalm—including words that have important implications for understanding the story as a whole.

In the psalm, the references to missing the Temple (v. 4) and being away from the land and the allusions to prison (v. 6) all suggest that this is a psalm from the period after the exile—perhaps when the people in the diaspora lamented their fate as exiles from the homeland. There are many other occasions when the exilic period is compared to living "in prison" (Isa. 42:7; Ps. 107:10-16; Lam. 3:34). So it seems clear that Jonah derives much of its power and meaning by being read "in diaspora" or "after the Exile." And this is the major clue to our interpretation of the story of Jonah. From this, we move to a direct consideration of the events of the tale itself.

Jonah's oracle of judgment against the "King" of Nineveh invites a most interesting response. This king descends from a symbol of his authority—the throne—and removes the symbol of his authority—his robe—and engages in the classic signs of mourning and sadness—putting on sackcloth and ashes. The king then leads the entire city in this act of repentance and engages in an act of fasting and mourning. What is also particularly interesting is the phrase: "All shall turn from their evil ways, and from that violence that is in their hands" (3:8). In short, the Assyrians are not going to be like the old Assyrians anymore. Here is a regime that forswears its weaponry and power, the "violence of their hands." Note that the "Ninevites" conduct the same kinds of acts of repentance noted in the more positive "procession of the nations" themes in other biblical passages that we have previously noted.

This phrase calls on us to consider other uses in the Bible of "violence of hands." In the Psalms, for example, hands that deal violence are kings and rulers:

> **Psalm 58:1-3:** Do you indeed decree what is right, you gods? Do you judge people fairly? No, in your hearts you devise wrongs; your *hands deal out violence* on earth. The wicked go astray from the womb; they err from their birth, speaking lies.

In other words, repentance means not merely a change of heart—but a change of behavior. Clearly, if the Ninevites are to be spared by God, they must repent of the violence of their rule. Furthermore, God recognizes that they have turned from their evil ways—and the implication is that they have turned from the ways of empire with its violence and destruction.

The delightful (and at the same time, profound) irony is that Jonah is furious at the compassion of God. It was, of course, this same divine compassion that saved his sodden hide from drowning in the sea, but now that God is showing compassion to an *enemy*, well, it's just too much (cf. Matt. 18:23-35 for a similar sentiment). The writer of the tale of Jonah relishes the border crossing that she/he is engaged in with this marvelous story, for the satire of Jonah's hatred offers a serious critique of the Hebrews who will be angered to see themselves ridiculed in the mirror of Jonah's attitudes.

There is no escaping the power of this tale, although many have tried to tone down its criticism of self-centered thinking. This is no book for narrowminded patriots who love only their own people. The book of Jonah is about God's compassion toward all people—even non-Hebrews. God cares for their well-being and for their transformation from the ways of destruction to the ways of life. But there is more to be said.

I am of the opinion, shared by other biblical scholars, that the story of Jonah is, in fact, a parable with a double meaning. Let us consider the facts:

- Jonah is called by God;
- rejects the call;
- is swallowed by the fish;
- and is then sent on a mission of deliverance for the Ninevites (even if reluctantly).

If we consider these themes: Called by God—Rejects the Call—Sent into Darkness—Released to a Mission, we begin to recognize a familiar theme. This is, of course, the general historical theme of the Bible itself, especially as represented by the preaching of Jeremiah and particularly the historical narrative that includes 1–2 Samuel and 1–2 Kings. The theme is that Israel was called by God, but sinfully rejected the call and listened to its own voices, after which the people were sent into exile (precisely what is warned against in Deuteronomy 28, as well as arguably the central message of the prophet Jeremiah). So what is the result of this exile—this "darkness" in the "big fish" (Jon. 2:5-6, "I went down to the land, whose bars closed upon me forever")? It is nothing less than the radical redefinition of what it means to be the people of God. The call now is to be a missionary people—with a peaceful mission even to the former enemies. The big fish, in other words, is the exile.

If this is true, let us cautiously come to understand the symbolic power of this tale—Jonah is a symbol of Israel itself—the one called to be the messenger to the world, the agent of God's "salvation to the ends of the earth." But Jonah is reluctant. According to the historical perspective of the books of Samuel and Kings, it was Israel's sin and rejection of God's laws that sent Israel into exile. According to Isaiah 49:6, however, it is precisely *during* the exile that some of the Hebrews came to understand the profound nature of their call in the world.

Jonah is to be read as a parable not only on the psalm/poem included in chapter 2, but most importantly, a parable written around the profound insights of Isaiah 49:6. It is a story that illustrates the radical call to be a "light to the nations." Even more intriguing, however, is the distinct probability that the story of Jonah was also inspired by two striking images in the teaching of Jeremiah. In Jeremiah 29, the prophet proposes that God actually sent the exiles to Babylon and that perhaps some good can come of it, even for the people of that city: "But seek the welfare of the city *where I have sent you* into exile, and pray to the LORD on its behalf, for in its welfare you will find your welfare" (Jer. 29:7). Equally striking is Jeremiah's image of the Exile itself:

Jeremiah 51:34: King Nebuchadrezzar of Babylon has devoured me, he has crushed me; he has made me an empty vessel, *he has swallowed me like a monster; he has filled his belly with my delicacies, he has spewed me out.*

Where do we go from here in our analysis of new thinking in the Exile?

THE "TWO PATHS" FROM THE EXILE INTO THE FUTURE

With the Exile comes a furious debate among Hebrews with regard to the future of God's people—would it be a future of returning to the land, regaining power, and trying once again to be a "nation like the other nations"? Would it then include conquering and humiliating the former "others," the nations? Or is there some radically new vision of what it means to be the people of God—something that involves being a "light to the nations"?

I would refer to this debate as "the two roads" that lead from the exilic experience in the scriptural tradition. One "road" leads back to a vision of restoration of power and then revenge against enemies. The other road clearly leads to a transformation of the enemy into something radically new—a potential partner with us in the kingdom of God. Incidentally, there is an interesting discussion in scholarly literature about whether the Assyrians are portrayed as actually "converting" in the book of Jonah, or whether they simply repent and come to recognize their sin before the God of the universe. If it is the latter, then they are considered acceptable *as Assyrians*. Isaiah 19:25 might suggest the latter. Either way—either by transforming the enemy into a partner in faith or engaging in dialogue so that the enemy becomes a partner in cooperation, we return to our guiding values of "mission" and/or "dialogue." Either interpretation of Jonah depends, however, on the courage of coyotes who risk running the borders of national hatreds and vengeance to seek new cooperation and new levels of communal relations with "others."

It would not be difficult to trace these two roads as they continue to lead to restoration of power and revenge on the one hand or transformation of the enemy on the other hand. A vengeful passage like Psalm 137 can obviously lead directly into the fury of 1 Maccabees and declaring wars of faith. But there is the other biblical road—a trail into wild territory filled with new challenges to meet the "other," and to risk new dreams and new hopes. This other road leads in a more difficult direction. It means, however, that some borders will be crossed.This is the road of transformation and reconciliation, and it may involve speaking difficult truths to the nations as Jonah did, and like Jonah, crossing some difficult borders in the process. Are there other signs of this biblical border running? Indeed there are.

Chapter Four

Crossing Over for Peace:
Two Hebrew "Coyotes"
Swim the "Rio Jordan"

In the last chapter, we considered two coyotes in the Hebrew tradition whose work arose from the devastation of exile and the angry rhetoric of the majority. The first was a voice that seems to call for a different attitude toward the nations in the book of Isaiah. Scholars call this voice Second Isaiah, meaning additional material (found mostly in chapters 40–66) added to the older book of Isaiah (mostly chapters 1–39). In some of these materials, we saw definite signs of a radically new approach to the nations, specifically summarized in the call to be "a light to the nations." While Jeremiah, who wrote at the very beginning of the Exile, might have influenced this new voice in Isaiah, the writer or writers of the Second Isaiah material took the idea of crossing borders between "us" and "them" much further. We then suggested that the story of Jonah is a brilliant, ironic, and certainly powerful call to further consider this unique approach.

It is fair to ask, however, whether this Hebrew "peace theology" continued beyond the years of the Exile and its immediate aftermath. In this chapter we will give voice to two more coyotes who continued to agitate for nonviolence and change. In each case, however, we will need to set the stage so that we can understand why these voices were so unique and important.

Two longstanding conflicts in the Old Testament involved Israel's festering relations with neighboring peoples across the Jordan. Relations between the Israelites and two of these neighbors—namely Edom and Moab—were often violent. In order to grasp the full impact of the Hebrew border crossers whom we will meet in this chapter, we need to briefly examine Israel's history with these two neighboring peoples.

EDOM AND MOAB: RUNNING ANOTHER BIBLICAL BORDER

The peoples known in the Bible as Edomites on the one hand, and the peoples known as Moabites on the other, are normally located by modern historians to the territories southeast of the Dead Sea for Edom, and territories just north of this known as the Plains of Moab. In short, we are speaking of neighbors across the Jordan.

Archaeologists suggest that Edom and Moab as place names are first known to the Egyptians already in the thirteenth century BCE, and were clearly cited as political entities from the time of the Neo-Assyrian Empire (roughly 900–650 BCE).

In the case of Moab, we have a particularly important testament to their political significance—an inscription from the Moabite ruler "Mesha," known as the "Mesha Inscription." This famous inscription calls for the practice of *herem* (that is, the massacre of all living beings) against the town of Nebo, in a battle against Israel.[1]

In many ways, both Edom and Moab were established in prime geographical locations. One of the most important trade routes in the entire region was the "King's Highway" which ran from the ports of the Red Sea (especially at the Gulf of Aqaba) up through the rift valleys, on past the Dead Sea, and then on north to Damascus and beyond—in other words, directly through Edomite and then into Moabite territory before heading north. Control of trade routes was obviously a lucrative business opportunity. Not only did the Assyrian Empire deal with the Edomites in this area as business partners but also the later Persian Empire dealt in the same area with the Qedarites, and even later, the Hellenistic and Roman empires dealt with the Nabataeans in precisely the same area. Whether these were names for descendants of the same people, we do not know—but they are peoples who populated the same lucrative geographical location in different eras. The Jewish ruler of the Greek period, John Hyrcanus, tried to convert by force the Idumeans (Edomites) in his kingdom, which would be an act that returned to haunt the descendants of the Judeans because Herod the Great would be a cruel descendant among these violently converted Idumeans. Collecting fees for passage, selling supplies, engaging in trade along the way—just imagine the significance of railroads in American history and how these "trade routes" literally created towns and cities along the way. Similar economic growth would accompany settlements along major trade routes which serviced (and taxed) the caravans passing through.

It seems obvious, then, that any kings of Israel and Judah would have an interest in conquering these regions so that they could control not only the trade along the sea route (where there was competition from the Philistines) but also the inland trade routes as well (1 Sam. 14:47; 2 Sam. 8:12; the taunt in Ps. 60:8 and 108:9; and Isa. 11:14 and predictions of conquest, etc.). Thus, in both cases, for Edom and for Moab, we have biblical evidence of territorial conflicts and disagreements over title and possession of land. What is particularly fascinating in the cases of Edom and Moab, however, is evidence for different opinions about these foreign peoples and places within the various books of the Bible.

What we know is that the Judeans in the west had jealous eyes for Edomite territory to their east. And the envy was mutual. In two of the "Arad Inscriptions" discovered in archaeological digs by Aharoni in 1962 and 1967 (no. 24 and no. 40) Edom is mentioned by Judeans in a context of hostility, and if the transcription is correct, Inscription no. 40 refers to an attempt by Judeans to prevent "the evil of the Edomites."[2] These inscriptions are dated near 597 BCE, the last days of independent Judea, when Edom may have seen an opportunity to push westward for more favorable lands and for trade routes toward the Mediterranean.

There is even an Edomite religious shrine that has been discovered in what was probably considered former Judean territory. There are archaeological inscriptions showing Moab's anger toward Israel, as well, such as the famous "Mesha Inscription" from a ninth-century Moabite ruler. Bruce Routledge, in *Moab in the Iron Age*, states the Moabite King Mesha's call to practice the "herem" in the disputed town of Nebo in the ninth century was as much an economic and political statement as it was a tactic of war. By devoting booty to destruction and killing a town's inhabitants, then no trade or sharing of resources or cooperation is allowed. Mesha declared his independence and his existence as a force to be reckoned with against Israelite territorial interests.[3]

When we turn to the Bible, the heated anger directed toward both the Edomites and the Moabites can be heard rather clearly (for Edom, especially, most prominently Ezekiel 25, Jeremiah 49, Lam. 4:21-22, and Psalm 137 and against Moab in Isaiah 16 and Jeremiah 48).

When did this begin? In the narrative of David's conquests (2 Sam. 8:13-14; 1 Kings 11:15-16; the title of Psalm 60; and parallel accounts in 1 Chronicles) the treatment of the Edomites indicated in these passages (allowing for exaggerated numbers) is brutal. Edom is again attacked by Amaziah of Judah: "He killed ten thousand Edomites in the Valley of Salt" (2 Kings 14:7). There were times, however, when Edom successfully resisted Judean control. The Bible notes the freedom of Edom from Judean control "in the days of King Joram of Israel and King Jehoram of Judah":

> **2 Kings 8:20-22:** In his days [referring to Jehoram] Edom revolted against the rule of Judah, and set up a king of their own. Then Joram crossed over to Zair with all his chariots. He set out by night and attacked the Edomites and their chariot commanders who had surrounded him; but his army fled home. So Edom has been in revolt against the rule of Judah to this day.[4]

The evidence of conflict is clear.

When we turn to the prophets, the anger against both nations continues. Typical of the prophetic condemnations of Edom and Moab are the accusations found in the "Oracles against the Nations" in Amos, where Edom appears to be specifically accused of participation in slave running:

> **Amos 1:9:** Thus says the LORD: For three transgressions of Tyre, and for four, I will not revoke the punishment; because they delivered entire communities over to Edom, and did not remember the covenant of kinship.

> **Amos 1:11:** Thus says the LORD: For three transgressions of Edom, and for four, I will not revoke the punishment; because he pursued his brother with the sword and cast off all pity; he maintained his anger perpetually, and kept his wrath forever.

Surely the most significant accusation made against Edom, however, is that they somehow participated in the destruction of Jerusalem in 587. Obadiah consists entirely of a condemnation of Edom. Particularly significant are verses 11 to 15:

> **Obadiah 11–15:** On the day that you stood aside, on the day that strangers carried off his wealth, and foreigners entered his gates and cast lots for Jerusalem, you too were like one of them. But you should not have gloated over your brother on the day of his misfortune; you should not have rejoiced over the people of Judah on the day of their ruin; you should not have boasted on the day of distress. You should not have entered the gate of my people on the day of their calamity; you should not have joined in the gloating over Judah's disaster on the day of his calamity; you should not have looted his goods on the day of his calamity. You should not have stood at the crossings to cut off his fugitives; you should not have handed over his survivors on the day of distress. For the day of the LORD is near against all the nations. As you have done, it shall be done to you; your deeds shall return on your own head.

It is a direct result of these condemnations of Edom in the prophetic material (cf. Isaiah 34; Isaiah 63:1; Jeremiah 49; Ezekiel

25; Ezekiel 35–36; and as late as Malachi 1:4) that many commentators have spoken of a special hatred for the Edomites, with some scholars actually suggesting that Edom was "historically . . . Israel's greatest enemy."[5] This is debatable, but the biblical heat generated by this rivalry is obvious.

Feelings toward Moab can also be quite heated in the prophets. Consider the viciousness of Isaiah's taunt that seems, at first, to call for sympathy for Moabites and then finishes by denying the suffering Moabites any sanctuary:

> **Isaiah 16:2-5:** Like fluttering birds, like scattered nestlings, so are the daughters of Moab at the fords of the Arnon. "Give counsel, grant justice; make your shade like night at the height of noon; hide the outcasts, do not betray the fugitive; let the outcasts of Moab settle among you; be a refuge to them from the destroyer." When the oppressor is no more, and destruction has ceased, and marauders have vanished from the land, then a throne shall be established in steadfast love in the tent of David, and on it shall sit in faithfulness a ruler who seeks justice and is swift to do what is right.

But it appears that this appeal for clemency and mercy is denied:

> **Isaiah 16:6, 7a, 11-14:** We have heard of the pride of Moab—how proud he is!—of his arrogance, his pride, and his insolence; his boasts are false. Therefore let Moab wail, let everyone wail for Moab. . . . Therefore my heart throbs like a harp for Moab, and my very soul for Kir-heres. When Moab presents himself, when he wearies himself upon the high place, when he comes to his sanctuary to pray, he will not prevail. This was the word that the LORD spoke concerning Moab in the past. But now the LORD says, In three years, like the years of a hired worker, the glory of Moab will be brought into contempt, in spite of all its great multitude; and those who survive will be very few and feeble.

Jeremiah also contains a strong condemnation of the Moabites. It seems that part of this anger is about Moab's comforts when Israel was suffering:

Jeremiah 48:9-12: Set aside salt for Moab, for she will surely fall; her towns shall become a desolation, with no inhabitant in them. Accursed is the one who is slack in doing the work of the LORD; and accursed is the one who keeps back the sword from bloodshed. Moab has been at ease from his youth, settled like wine on its dregs; he has not been emptied from vessel to vessel, nor has he gone into exile; therefore his flavor has remained and his aroma is unspoiled. Therefore, the time is surely coming, says the LORD, when I shall send to him decanters to decant him, and empty his vessels, and break his jars in pieces.

Jeremiah uses the reputation of Moabite wine production to further his taunt against them:

Jeremiah 48:26-31: Make him drunk, because he magnified himself against the LORD; let Moab wallow in his vomit; he too shall become a laughingstock. Israel was a laughingstock for you, though he was not caught among thieves; but whenever you spoke of him you shook your head. Leave the towns, and live on the rock, O inhabitants of Moab. Be like the dove that nests on the sides of the mouth of a gorge. We have heard of the pride of Moab—he is very proud—of his loftiness, his pride, and his arrogance, and the haughtiness of his heart. I myself know his insolence, says the LORD; his boasts are false, his deeds are false. Therefore I wail for Moab; I cry out for all Moab; for the people of Kir-heres I mourn.

Such voices give us the impression that there is a united biblical voice against Edomites and Moabites, among others. But such an impression would be hasty, to say the least.

ALTERNATIVE VOICES OF COMPASSION?

Now we arrive at a mystery. The fact of the matter is that the biblical records about Edom and Moab are not entirely of one voice on the matter of relations with both peoples. There is a perplexing difference of opinion in the Bible with regard to these neighbors to the east.

Beginning with the tradition about the wilderness wandering, Numbers 20:14-21 "remembers" the occasion when the Edomites *refused* to allow Moses and the exodus entourage passage through Edomite territory. The passage concludes: "Thus Edom refused to give Israel passage through their territory; so Israel turned away from them" (Num. 20:21). This negative attitude seems quite compatible with the negative views expressed in the other texts we have examined. Similarly with Moab, the tradition in Numbers "remembers" that Moab also refused the Israelites any assistance and recounts the extended tradition that King Balak tried to have the Israelites officially cursed by Balaam. But when we turn to Deuteronomy, on the contrary, it states clearly that the Israelites most certainly *did* pass through the territory of the Edomites "their kin" (the Hebrew term is actually "your brother") and furthermore, contains a strong endorsement of Edomite rights to their land:

> **Deuteronomy 2:4-6:** And charge the people as follows: You are about to pass through the territory of your kindred, the descendants of Esau, who live in Seir. They will be afraid of you, so, be very careful not to engage in battle with them, for I will not give you even so much as a foot's length of their land, since I have given Mount Seir to Esau as a possession. You shall purchase food from them for money, so that you may eat; and you shall also buy water from them for money, so that you may drink.

In the case of Moab, also, a different memory is suggested:

> **Deuteronomy 2:8b-9:** When we had headed out along the route of the wilderness of Moab, the LORD said to me: "Do not harass Moab or engage them in battle, for I will not give you any of its land as a possession, since I have given Ar as a possession to the descendants of Lot."

What seems particularly noteworthy in the comparison of these passages is precisely the suggestion of trade and relations between the peoples. In the case of Edom, Moses offered to pay for anything they used, yet according to Numbers they were turned down flat. Yet, the people are strictly told to **pay** for whatever they use in the account in Deuteronomy. It seems inescapable that the two Edom passages are related—representing differing assessments of the relationship to the Edomites. Deuteronomy further confirms this difference in the passage in 23:7: "You shall not abhor any of the Edomites, for they are your kin" (again, literally "your brothers"). As we have seen in the case of Moab, there appears to be some hope for a positive future relationship hinted in Deuteronomy as well (especially ironic, in relation to Deut. 23:3). Yet another disagreement?

So what explains the difference of opinion? It might be the influence of Hebrew coyotes—wildcat storytellers and peacemakers who dare to imagine a different relationship with the people who are supposed to be "the enemy." Let us see if we can hear their voices in the stories of Jacob for Edom and the story of Ruth for Moab.

CHALLENGING THE HATRED OF EDOM: THE STORY OF TWO BROTHERS: JACOB AND ESAU

Recent trends in scholarship on Genesis suggest that many of the stories of Genesis were written or edited much later in Israelite history than previously thought. It is now quite common to suggest that the Adam/Eve story of being "exiled" from the garden reflects on the Babylonian Exile and that other stories that may have had older roots were reworked after the crisis of 587 BCE. If that is the case, then something quite striking happens when the Jacob stories are reread in this post-587 context. The stories of Genesis provide fascinating views of certain peoples known to the Hebrews. Some of the characters of the stories are said to be the founders of a nation—like Ishmael and the tribes of "Ishmaelites." The way some of these stories are told, we can guess that opinions of some of these other nations were not exactly flattering. Consider, for example, the biblical opinion that the Moabites and Ammonites are said to be the descendents of incestuous sexual intercourse between Lot and his daughters (Gen. 19:36-38).

Similarly, Genesis associates Edom with Esau, the brother of Jacob. Genesis 36:8 flatly states: "Esau is Edom." Certainly in later biblical thought, this tradition of associating Edom with Esau is well established (Gen. 25:30; 32:3; 36:1,8,19; and Obadiah.) The importance of this will be clarified in a moment—for now let us simply follow the story of Jacob and Esau in the book of Genesis.

Genesis 25:24-34 begins the cycle of Jacob and Esau stories, establishing the conflict between the two brothers. In chapter 25, Jacob cooks a "red" stew, the color quite probably a play on the term for "Edom" (Edom means "red"). When Jacob cooks the meal, he apparently knows that his brother Esau would be hungry—and with this temptation blackmails Esau into agreeing to forsake his birthright for food. Many commentators on the Bible have suggested, somewhat unfairly, that Esau was an idiot, and many attempt to blame Esau for being easily tricked and for so easily giving up his birthright simply because he was hungry. But Christopher Heard has pointed out that if Esau is truly at the point of collapse from exhaustion, then Esau is right. What good are his birthrights if he is dead?[6]

Many readers of Genesis try to present Esau as dim-witted precisely to avoid the observation that Jacob would otherwise be cast in a considerably more negative light for his virtual threat of negligence at his brother's collapse and death from exhaustion. So, to avoid Jacob being implicated in murder, many readers of Genesis try to portray Esau in as negative a light as possible so as to excuse Jacob's trickery as little more than sibling rivalry. Recent scholarly comments are somewhat shocking, referring to Esau as: "slow-witted ... thoughtless ... impulsive ... a block-head"[7]; "unsophisticated, unthinking oaf"[8]; "unpolished ... callous"[9]; a "stupid man ... limited intelligence."[10] But this abuse of Esau ought not to excuse Jacob simply because he is the heir to the promises of God. In any case, Esau makes the deal, and in the end he is saved by eating the meal.

What the storytellers set up in 25:29-34 is then consummated in chapter 27, when Jacob (now, it seems, unable to cook for himself) uses his mother's second pot of stew to fool the elder father Isaac into giving Jacob the blessing clearly intended for Esau. The

"Blessing of the Father" is critically important—it is basically passing on to the son the responsibilities and rights as head of the family. Jacob, pretending to be his brother Esau, is thus given "the richness of the earth." But in the blessing given to Esau, after Jacob steals the original blessing, Isaac delivers an interesting sting at the end:

> **Genesis 27:39:** Then his father Isaac answered him: "See, away from the fatness of the earth shall your home be, and away from the dew of heaven on high. By your sword you shall live, and you shall serve your brother; but when you break loose, you shall break his yoke from your neck."

It is virtually universal among commentators on Genesis that we are to read into this blessing both the conquest of Edom by David (2 Sam. 8:13-14; 1 Kings 11:15-16; the title of Psalm 60; and parallel accounts in 1 Chron. 18:12) and the eventual revolt of Edom from Judean control in the time of Jehoram (2 Kings 8:20-22). So, it seems, the writer of this story in Genesis is aware of both the Davidic conquest of Edom and the break from Judean control.

Commentators like Claus Westermann have pointed out that the story of Jacob's theft of Esau's blessing is unparalleled in its dramatic effects—dwelling on the emotional reactions of both Isaac and especially Esau, as at the moment when Jacob's betrayal is discovered by his brother: "When Esau heard his father's words, he cried out with an exceedingly great and bitter cry, and said to his father, 'Bless me, me also, father' " (Gen. 27:34, cf. v. 38, and of Isaac—v. 33). The result is that Esau "hated Jacob," and planned for a time when "I will kill my brother Jacob" (v. 41).[11]

The blessing of lands—Jacob's "fatness of the earth" compared to Esau's location "away from the fatness of the earth"—suggests that what may be right "behind the story" of Jacob and Esau is rivalry about land. Are land disputes between Judah ("Jacob") and Edom ("Esau") symbolized in the blessing from Isaac?

If the story stopped here—everything would be clear. The reason why the story in Genesis (and all those passages later in the Bible) represents hatred between Judah and Edom is because of land disputes and an ancient rivalry that is thought to go "back to our forefathers." As we know from many conflicts throughout the world, ancient folklore about the origins of the conflict may not explain the actual beginning of the conflict, but often effectively continues to fan the flames of hatred and animosity. But we are not finished—there are other thoughts on the matter of Edom and Judah that appear in the biblical writings and even in Genesis.

After Jacob flees the anger of Esau, he must work for fourteen years for a relative, Laban. But when that time is finished, Jacob wishes to head "home" (that is, Israelite territory). The story states that Jacob's route forces him to face the possibility of meeting his estranged brother, Esau. Immediately, Jacob sends messengers, employing the interesting terminology of "Lord" in relation to Esau, and "servant" in relation to himself. Furthermore, although Jacob presents gifts (the Hebrew word is *minchot*) to Esau, eventually Jacob presents to Esau what he calls a blessing (the Hebrew word at that point is *beraka*). We thus come to a startling moment in the story because it was the blessing that Jacob stole from Esau in the first place. As a result of this act of restorative justice, the eventual reconciliation scene is striking:

> **Genesis 33:1-4:** Now Jacob looked up and saw Esau coming, and four hundred men with him. So he divided the children among Leah and Rachel and the two maids. He put the maids with their children in front, then Leah with her children, and Rachel and Joseph last of all. He himself went on ahead of them, bowing himself to the ground seven times, until he came near his brother. But Esau ran to meet him, and embraced him, and fell on his neck and kissed him, and they wept.

What has happened? Esau was said to be meeting Jacob with four hundred men (32:6), and Jacob was clearly terrified (32:7). Some scholars suggest that four hundred men means, quite simply, that Esau approached with an army. But there is no battle—there is rather an emotionally powerful reconciliation between enemies.

Not surprisingly, many scholars resist this conclusion, having a hard time accepting the radical implications of a storyteller suggesting that Judeans and Edomites could reconcile their longstanding hatreds. Some have even suggested that this reconciliation was really a diplomatic victory of Jacob over a still slow-witted Esau.

Roger Syren points out that Jacob's prayer in this story has clear associations with the Hebrew tradition of "penitential prayer," which includes confession of guilt and request for forgiveness. (The typical examples of the penitential prayer tradition are found in 1 Kings 8; Nehemiah 9; Ezra 9; Daniel 9; and Baruch).[12] If elements of the penitential prayer tradition are suggested in Genesis 32–33, then Jacob understood that justice must precede peace **and that he was guilty**. Jacob effectively "returns" the "blessing" stolen from Esau.

The writer of the Jacob story is suggesting that peace may actually follow justice. The fact that Edom and Judah have conflict over land—possibly stemming from Edom's encroachments into the Negev—suggests that the Jacob and Esau stories may well symbolize other economic and political issues between these two peoples. It is, therefore, hard to avoid the suggestion that the writer of Genesis 33 is either reflecting an accommodation between the Judean and Edomite peoples at some stage (an accommodation that we sadly cannot confirm with present evidence) *or the writer is a Hebrew coyote—flagrantly violating his own people's anger against the Edomites and "crossing borders" by advocating a new approach to the Edomites.*

Esau was not "tricked" or "appeased." Rather, justice was accomplished. Furthermore, the text leaves us in little doubt that Jacob was acting responsibly to initiate the reconciliation and to see that justice was done. His payment and his words are not clever stratagems or cynical tricks like the old Jacob we know; rather, Jacob faced the reality of injustice. In other words, the Jacob and Esau story provides us with a potent counterpoint to the other passages in scripture that reflect hatred toward Edom on the part of Israelites.

So much for the conflict with Edom. What about the conflict with Moab? Here, too, we can hear an alternative, border-crossing voice, if we but listen.

ANOTHER STORYTELLER AND RIVER RUNNER: RUTH VERSUS EZRA'S BORDER PATROL

The story of Ruth is a familiar one, and justifiably popular. Here is the story of a Moabite woman who marries into a Hebrew family while these Hebrews are living in Moab, across the Jordan River, to escape a famine in Judah. Tragically, all the males in the family die, leaving Naomi alone with her two Moabite daughters-in-law. Believing that this unlikely family composed of women from two cultures would not be a realistic arrangement (especially as there appear to be no children to make such an arrangement necessary), and also believing that her luck had simply run out (1:13b), Naomi bids farewell to her Moabite "daughters," and heads home to Judah. Naomi wishes to preserve "borders"—perhaps never approving of her son's marriages in the first place. If the story of Naomi and Ruth ended here, we might better understand the biblical hostility toward all things Moabite.

Our interest, however, focuses on Numbers 25, the chapter that describes a story known to many students of the Bible as The Incident at Baal-Peor. The story describes some of the Israelite peoples entering into mixed marriages with women of Moab. As a result, the story implies, many Israelites also began to follow their Moabite wives in local religious practices and specifically participating in the local religious worship of Baal—a regional fertility god known throughout this entire area. (Compare 1 Kings 3:1-2; 11:1-3; 14:21-24; 16:31-32.)

The solution to the problem is horrifically violent. Moses tells people to kill any member of their families who has become involved in the worship of Baal. But the connection with mixed marriage continues with the incident that is described in verses 6–11:

Numbers 25:6-11: Just then one of the Israelites came and brought a Midianite woman into his family, in the sight of Moses and in the sight of the whole congregation of the Israelites, while they were weeping at the entrance of the tent of meeting. When Phinehas son of Eleazar, son of Aaron the priest, saw it, he got up and left the congregation. Taking a spear in his hand, he went after the Israelite man into the tent, and pierced the two of them, the Israelite and the woman, through the belly. So the plague was stopped among the people of Israel. Nevertheless those that died by the plague were twenty-four thousand. The LORD spoke to Moses, saying: "Phinehas son of Eleazar, son of Aaron the priest, has turned back my wrath from the Israelites by manifesting such zeal among them on my behalf that in my jealousy I did not consume the Israelites."

Important in the description is the fact that mixed marriages are seen as potentially realigning social and political relations, and as such could be the source of serious social problems, and violence is thus seen as the solution in some cases ... not merely divorce. Crucial to understanding the hostility toward mixed marriage is the fact that the Bible sees such marriages as politically significant. Modern family therapists often warn young couples that part of the reality of their marriage will be the fact that two families are "marrying," not merely two individuals—and sometimes two cultures are "marrying." Marriages, in the Bible and in the ancient Near East, often symbolized political alliances, and thus all mixed marriages had potentially political and social significance. In short, mixed marriages symbolized the possibility that whole groups will be in a new relationship. Genesis 34 is thus a highly significant example of Jacob's sons rejecting this political and social realignment inherently implied in Dinah's proposed marriage.

This hostility toward intermarriage with the Moabites is carefully articulated:

Deuteronomy 23:3: No Ammonite or Moabite shall be admitted to the assembly of the LORD. Even to the tenth generation, none of their descendants shall be admitted to the assembly of the LORD.

This hostility toward Moabites, and especially as it is expressed in the context of the fear of mixed marriages, reaches its pinnacle during the crises after the destruction of Jerusalem in 586 and in the later post-exilic setting in the books of Ezra and Nehemiah.

Ezra and Nehemiah are two leaders of the Hebrew community who come from the far-flung settlements of the Hebrews some time after the Exile, and return to Jerusalem around 450 BCE to help out in various ways. But Ezra, a priest, is appalled to discover that some of the Hebrews have entered into marriages with foreign women.

> **Ezra 9:1-2:** After these things had been done, the officials approached me and said, "The people of Israel, the priests, and the Levites have not separated themselves from the peoples of the lands with their abominations, from the Canaanites, the Hittites, the Perizzites, the Jebusites, the Ammonites, the Moabites, the Egyptians, and the Amorites. For they have taken some of their daughters as wives for themselves and for their sons. Thus the holy seed has mixed itself with the peoples of the lands, and in this faithlessness the officials and leaders have led the way."

We can almost hear Ezra's anguished prayers across time:

> **Ezra 9:3-7:** When I heard this, I tore my garment and my mantle, and pulled hair from my head and beard, and sat appalled. Then all who trembled at the words of the God of Israel, because of the faithlessness of the returned exiles, gathered around me while I sat appalled until the evening sacrifice. At the evening sacrifice I got up from my fasting, with my garments and my mantle torn, and fell on my knees, spread out my hands to the LORD my God, and said, "O my God, I am too ashamed and embarrassed to lift my face to you, my God, for our iniquities have risen higher than our heads, and our guilt has mounted up to the heavens. From the days of our ancestors to this day we have been deep in guilt, and for our iniquities we, our kings, and our priests have been handed over to the kings of the lands, to the sword, to captivity, to plundering, and to utter shame, as is now the case."

The people's solution to Ezra's anguished concern over mixed marriage is as startling as it is thorough:

Ezra 10:2-5: "We have broken faith with our God and have married foreign women from the peoples of the land, but even now there is hope for Israel in spite of this. So now let us make a covenant with our God to send away all these wives and their children, according to the counsel of my lord and of those who tremble at the commandment of our God; and let it be done according to the law. Take action, for it is your duty, and we are with you; be strong, and do it." Then Ezra stood up and made the leading priests, the Levites, and all Israel swear that they would do as had been said. So they swore.

Ezra makes the people swear that they will be loyal to the borders between "them" and "us," and as the chapter ends, masses of women married to Israelite males are sent away. I suppose we ought to be thankful for the blessing that they were not murdered, as Phineas had done at the time of Moses, but the solution still seems extreme. The borders are clear—and they are agreed with by Ezra's compatriot, Nehemiah, who seems equally troubled by mixed marriages and even cites the Deuteronomy passage yet again:

Nehemiah 13:1, 3: On that day they read from the book of Moses in the hearing of the people; and in it was found written that no Ammonite or Moabite should ever enter the assembly of God.... When the people heard the law, they separated from Israel all those of foreign descent.

It seems that the borders are secure, but are they? People appear to be crossing the "Rio Jordan" in the night. In other words, Hebrew coyotes are active. The writer of the book of Ruth is one of them.

When we left our description of the book of Ruth, Naomi was speaking to her Moabite daughters-in-law, and telling them (in so many words) that this was just not going to work out. Perhaps Naomi was under the influence of the thinking associated with

Ezra's border patrol. One Moabite daughter (probably muttering something disparaging about male Israelite longevity) walks off. But Ruth is a surprise—she pleads with Naomi to allow her to remain by her side:

> **Ruth 1:16-18:** But Ruth said, "Do not press me to leave you or to turn back from following you. Where you go, I will go; where you lodge, I will lodge; your people shall be my people, and your God my God. Where you die, I will die—there will I be buried. May the LORD do thus and so to me, and more as well, if even death parts me from you." When Naomi saw that she was determined to go with her, she said no more to her.

The use of the twin phrase, "my people" and "my God," seems hardly accidental. It appears as the covenant phrase whereby God seals the relationship with the people of Israel:

> **Exodus 6:7:** I will take you as my people, and I will be your God.

> **Leviticus 26:12:** And I will walk among you, and will be your God, and you shall be my people.

Thus, the Hebrew coyote writing the book of Ruth presents a Moabite woman as acceptable, even heroic in her care for Naomi, and one who fully integrates into the Israelite people, even using the language of the covenant between God and God's people. But does the writer of Ruth consciously contradict what appears to be a law of Moses? It seems unavoidable to conclude that the writer of Ruth disagrees with Deuteronomy 23:3 that "no Ammonite or Moabite shall be admitted to the assembly of the Lord. Even to the tenth generation . . . "

We may even have an idea when this disagreement arose. The disputes about mixed marriage and defining the borders of "us" and "them" in the chaotic times after the Exile provide a logical context for the composition of this story. But the writer of Ruth, quite cleverly, sets the story far in the past, which is why the book appears near the book of Judges, which is the setting given to the story. Given the politically and socially loaded meaning of mixed marriages in the Bible, the writer of Ruth is clearly engaging in foreign policy (at the very least proposing radically altered social relationships with Moabites) and is not merely writing a sentimental romance novel for Israelite entertainment.

CONCLUSION

Two Hebrew coyotes are running the River Jordan by telling stories that challenge the status quo of hatred toward foreigners. For the majority, the River Jordan quite clearly forms an important boundary between "us" and "them." "They" are to be condemned, and there is clear evidence of hostilities between Judah and Israel on the one hand and Edom and Moab on the other. We even have textual evidence that the feelings were mutual. Edom and Moab clearly had hostile feelings toward the Judeans as well and even bragged about military brutalities with as much zest as the Bible can brag about committing such atrocities. King Mesha of Moab is obviously just as brutal and angry as the writer of Joshua or Ezra.

What is important, however, is that we have biblical voices that question the violent borders between peoples—coyotes who violate acceptable divisions—and propose that coexistence is possible. Furthermore, it seems hardly coincidental that the writer of the Jacob and Esau story places it in the context of land disputes between brothers, while the writer of Ruth chooses to take up the issue of mixed marriage. Mixed marriage was far more often part of the biblical disputes with Moab than it was with the traditions surrounding Edom. In short, our coyote writers attack the heart of the dispute in both cases: land with Edom and social relations with Moab.

We could go on; these are but two more examples. But the argument is now clear: we cannot simply listen to one "side" of the biblical arguments on these matters, and not allow other voices to speak. We need to learn the travel songs that are sung by these Hebrew storytellers and dissenters for peace. It may well be that the New Testament will take up the same tune originally sung by these voices of Hebrew border runners.

Chapter Five

The New "Creationism": Pray Globally—Act Nonviolently

I. GOD'S PEACEFUL CREATION

The Jewish biblical theologian Jon Levenson has observed that the parts of the Bible that speak most strikingly about *universalism* are those parts where God is most highly honored as the Creator. What we mean by universalism is found on those occasions when the biblical writers seem to ignore the differences between human beings and treat all peoples as God's creatures together. In other words, when they focus on God as Creator, they tend to forget about human borders. Look at a picture taken of the earth from space—from a "God's eye view," if you will. Where are the borders? They've disappeared.

The writings in the Bible that speak most extensively about God as Creator are found in two primary locations—the descriptions of the creation at the beginning of Genesis and those that appear in the Wisdom literature (Proverbs, Job, Ecclesiastes). So it seems hardly surprising that when creation and Wisdom literature speaks of God as the Creator, there is very little discussion of anything specifically Hebrew in these Biblical texts. It is more general, more universal, in its discussion of humanity and God.

What is even more interesting is that these creation and Wisdom traditions also have a very strong ethic of peacefulness.

It seems that the Wisdom tradition's emphasis on God as Creator contributes to a profound sense that from "God's point of view," our differences mean less, and our conflicts are even more ridiculous. And, as we shall see, the creation accounts feature some profound observations about human violence.

In this chapter, I bring together these two traditions—creation and Wisdom—in order to describe a new *creationism*. What I mean, of course, is a kind of biblical globalism, not a fundamentalist insistence that Genesis 1–2 are some kind of textbook lesson in astrophysics. The stories are far more profound than fundamentalism realizes. This is the kind of creationism that emphasizes our status as created beings, intended by God to live together in peace. It is a creationism that intentionally ignores borders for the sake of humanity at large.

In order to fully describe this new creationism, I will begin by considering the significance of the seven-day creation story. The old creationism thought that this story was important because it was supposed to be taken as a literal description of how the universe came to be—made by God in seven, twenty-four-hour periods. By insisting that people must all believe a particular way, this old creationism draws borders between those who believe "like us," and those who do not. Thus, it violates the very spirit of the new creationism, which is about thinking and praying on a global scale, so we can more faithfully work for change in our local communities.

THE SEVEN DAYS OF CREATION: "PLACING THOUGHTS AT THE BEGINNING"

Many of my friends in the Uniting Church of Australia have learned from their Christian brothers and sisters who are also members of the indigenous peoples of Australia.[1] One of the things they have learned about is the Aboriginal Australian idea of "the dreamtime," or the preferred term: "the dreaming." This is a concept that is traditional for some (but not all) of the Aboriginal Australian cultures. It is a concept of history that is at once difficult to understand but fascinating to consider. As I understand it from conversation and reading, the idea is that the past is not merely what has happened before us, but is also a living presence—it continues to impact how we live and think from another place. And in a particularly interesting thought, the past guides the future. For many Aboriginal Australians, "dreamings" are stories and understandings that guide their entire identity but are also associated with geographical features and physical places in the land that carry special meaning. This is profoundly similar to what many historians of ancient civilizations believe about the role of ancient stories (especially those ancient peoples surrounding the people of the Bible). The ancient stories of a society influence their ideas of reality. Richard Clifford, a scholar who has worked extensively on early creation stories of ancient peoples surrounding the people of the Bible, states that the ancients believed that "the originating moment explains the present. That moment grounds or explains something experienced here and now—the sacredness of a temple, the status of a god, the authority of a king."[2]

As a visitor to Australia and an interested amateur who reads about modern Aboriginal Australian issues when I can, I became especially fascinated with the concept of "the dreaming" as a way of thinking about the significance of the book of Genesis. Like "the dreaming" for modern Aboriginal Australians, the stories of Genesis are a reflection of more than merely Hebrew reflections on their origins. I believe that these stories seem to reflect thoughts from many different times in Hebrew history, including the period after 587 and the destruction of Jerusalem, and I will further argue that placing a story "first" means that a very significant claim is being made about the enduring significance of that story.

We are now quite familiar with the idea that final written products can be composed in sections, and then rearranged, rather like filming a movie in separate shoots that are only placed in order by a final editor. In our day of modern media and computer word processing, it is easier for us to realize the significance of the observation that what appears "earlier" in the Bible is not necessarily the passages that were written first. Sometimes it is a very good question to ask why a particular passage was placed where it is, especially if it seems possible that it may not have been there in earlier versions. But to be clear, the purpose of these questions is not to propose that the "original form" was somehow better or more accurate, but rather to suggest that there is some significance to placing something in strategic locations—such as at the beginning, or the end, or in regular intervals throughout. Thinking about the placement of texts potentially contributes to our understanding.

For example, biblical scholars have been rather certain for some time now that the seven-day creation story that begins the book of Genesis (the story that does not feature Adam and Eve but rather presents males and females as being created at the same time) was probably written after 587 and perhaps quite a while after the older Adam and Eve story. The seven-day story, however, was "placed" just before the Adam and Eve story—as we have it in the present form of the book of Genesis. Scholars disagree as to the precise times when these two stories were composed, or at least written down, but the relative order of the two stories (the seven-day story is more recent, the Adam and Eve story somewhat older) seems widely accepted. So, a passage appearing first does not mean it is the oldest. And, of course, first does not even necessarily mean most important. Furthermore, the idea of editing the writings that would eventually become parts of our Bible need not interfere with the idea of the Bible as revelation, since human beings are the ones writing down what they believe God is telling them, and it seems perfectly reasonable for writers of these works to realize later that things could be said better, more clearly, or with more impact. I find it entirely strange for some conservative Christians to insist that only the first writing is inspired, but later editing never can be. I would argue that editors can be inspired.

Let us get to the point, which is precisely to ask: what was the editor of the final form of the opening stories of Genesis intending to communicate to readers of the Genesis scroll by placing the "seven days" of creation at the very beginning? Let us first think about the Adam and Eve tradition.

The Adam and Eve stories, as they presently read, begin with an ideal picture of the creation of the first human being, followed by creatures, and then eventually a woman for a companion. But conflict begins almost immediately after the initial work of creation is finished. Chapter 3 takes a clear emotional turn—an adversary is introduced in the serpent, questions are raised, and the violation of the intended order takes place. Creation is divided into warring factions—people are set against God, animals against people (Gen. 3:15). Some have observed that the Adam and Eve story functions almost like an origin story for human troubles and separations—humanity from God, male and female from each other, brother against brother, and people against people. The clear impression from this account is that humanity is deeply flawed, and while it may not have started this way, it most certainly ends up being a harsh world. Animals are "cursed" (Gen. 3:14), the ground is "cursed" (Gen 3:17), and Cain is "cursed" (Gen. 4:11). Is this the status of the world? Cursed by insurmountable borders between ourselves and God, the rest of creation and ourselves, and even from each other? Is "exile from the garden" our final state? Are our lives to be endlessly composed of alienation and conflict? Such questions were answered by a strikingly creative preacher from sometime after the Exile who added another story just before the Adam and Eve accounts of human flaws. Why add a passage dealing with seven days of creation?

WHERE'S THE BATTLE? GENESIS 1 AS PREACHING PEACE

One of the most important things that is said in the seven-day creation story is how God created. I don't mean to say "how" in the sense of the physics of creation. I leave that to the paleobiologists and astrophysicists to work out. The Bible is neither a physics nor a biology textbook. The writers of the seven-day creation story, however, most certainly are interested in "how" God created in one very important way: God created alone, and God created in peace.[3]

There is profound importance to the notion suggested by Genesis 1 that peace is the created order—conflict is not "hard wired" into the very fabric of created order. In other words, peace is the intended and underlying theme of God's actions. This is a potent challenge to anyone who would argue that violence is the "natural way," and that conflict is "just how we are." Genesis 1 flatly denies this destructive notion. Consider, once again, the opening lines:

> **Genesis 1:1:** In the beginning when God created the heavens and the earth, the earth was a formless void and darkness covered the face of the deep, while a wind from God swept over the face of the waters. Then God said, "Let there be light"; and there was light. And God saw that the light was good; and God separated the light from the darkness. God called the light Day, and the darkness he called Night. And there was evening and there was morning, the first day.

When we hear or read these words, we tend to read this as modern, technologically sophisticated people who are interested in the scientific issues—we want to know about chemistry, physics, and biology. Or perhaps we are interested in poetry or the way in which ancient writers conceive of the cosmos. In any case, it is arguable that we do not react like an ancient Canaanite, or ancient Babylonian, or an ancient Egyptian would react if *they* heard this story. It is also the case that their reactions (if we could reproduce what they may have thought) would tell us volumes because they may have been the intended audience.

From what we know about the mythologies and ideas of creation from these ancient societies, I propose that a typical Canaanite or Babylonian would listen to a Hebrew telling the story of the seven days of creation, and would react with some disappointment and immediately ask, "What? That's it? Where is the battle?" What battle are they talking about? This is precisely the key to understanding Genesis 1.

When these ancient peoples spoke of creation, they thought rather dramatically different things about how creation came about and how people came to exist. And, they clearly provoked the writer of the seven-day story. We know this, at least to some degree of confidence, partly because many of their ancient creation stories have survived and have been translated and also because the Bible so often refers or alludes to those ancient texts. What is interesting about most of these stories is not so much the details of how they differ from one another, but what is similar in virtually **all** of them—including those of the Canaanites who lived near and among the Hebrews. When we speak of "Canaanite mythology," we are really speaking of the general culture surrounding the Hebrews, with similar versions among Egyptians, Babylonians, Assyrians—throughout the entire region.

What we are interested in is the fact that there is a singular idea that seems shared among many of these cultures and peoples: the notion that the creation of humanity and human civilization resulted from a cosmic battle between the gods. Let us briefly summarize their ideas about creation from divine conflict.

THE COMBAT MYTH OF THE ANCIENT NEAR EAST

Scholars refer to this generally similar notion as the *Combat Myth*. The importance of the Combat Myth for readers of Genesis, however, is precisely its absence, or perhaps better, its reformulation, in the Bible. So, it is important to know something about what is missing in the Bible, not only because it is not there, but also because the biblical writers leave all kinds of hints and allusions to the Combat Myth, telling us that they knew it very well indeed (Ps. 74:12-17, etc.). In other words, clearly the biblical writers wanted us to know that the Combat Myth's absence in Genesis was a matter of intention, rather than ignorance. Surveying the various cultural expressions of the ancient Combat Myth in many different ancient mythologies, we can point out that it shares similar themes and list them as follows:

- a force, often depicted as a monster, threatens the cosmic or political order;
- the threat instills fear among the other gods;

- unable to find an older god willing to take on the monster/threat, the assembly turns to a younger god to battle the hostile force;
- he successfully defeats the monster, often creating the world and human beings as a part of his success.[4]

It is particularly significant to note, however, that the monster who threatens order is often associated with the sea, and the young hero god is associated with the storm. In Canaanite versions of the myth that we now know of, Baal is the hero god and is associated with the storm (which means that his power is associated with winds, he uses lightning, his voice is like thunder, etc.). Yam, the serpentine monster, is portrayed as a sea monster. Professor Mark Smith, who has worked extensively with the Baal texts from the ancient Canaanite city of Ugarit, writes, "The struggles of Baal mirror the struggles of humanity against the vicissitudes of a dangerous world, but the victories of Baal also herald the divine victory, which reinvigorates not only the world of the divine pantheon but also human society."[5]

In the ancient Babylonian version of this same Combat Myth known as "Enuma Elish," Marduk is the young hero, and Tiamat is the sea god. Many scholars have suggested that Marduk represents the forces of order and civilization, and, therefore, "fights" to overcome disorder and chaos represented by the coiling sea monster, Tiamat.

The interesting question is—did the Hebrews also know about these traditions? Were they aware of the great Combat Myth that was the basis of human creation or at least the basis of the order of human society and the cosmos? It would seem logical that the Canaanite Baal/Yam myths would be known to the Hebrews who lived among the Canaanites. Do we have evidence that they knew these stories and traditions? The clear answer is yes—many biblical texts indicate that the Hebrews most certainly did know about these traditions. For example, the Canaanite mythology is alluded to, hinted at, and referred to frequently in biblical poetry, and especially Psalms. Some of the more famous examples include Psalm

77:13-20, which begins with a praise of God, but quickly leads into a familiar set of images contrasting storm and sea:

> **Psalm 77:13-20:** Your way, O God, is holy. What god is so great as our God? You are the God who works wonders; you have displayed your might among the peoples. With your strong arm you redeemed your people, the descendants of Jacob and Joseph. *Selah*. When the waters saw you, O God, when the waters saw you, they were afraid; the very deep trembled. The clouds poured out water; the skies thundered; your arrows flashed on every side. The crash of your thunder was in the whirlwind; your lightnings lit up the world; the earth trembled and shook. Your way was through the sea, your path, through the mighty waters; yet your footprints were unseen. You led your people like a flock by the hand of Moses and Aaron.

Similarly, in Psalm 97, storm images are used in relation to the power of Yahweh, the God of the Hebrews:

> **Psalm 97:2-5:** Clouds and thick darkness are all around him; righteousness and justice are the foundation of his throne. Fire goes before him, and consumes his adversaries on every side. His lightnings light up the world; the earth sees and trembles. The mountains melt like wax before the LORD, before the Lord of all the earth.

The book of Job also very clearly alludes to the Canaanite Combat Myth:

> **Job 26:12-13:** By his power he stilled the Sea; by his understanding he struck down Rahab. By his wind the heavens were made fair; his hand pierced the fleeing serpent.

My personal favorite among these references to Canaanite religious mythology, however, is Isaiah 51, where the conflict between the storm and the sea is mixed with the history of the Exodus (a connection already established in Exodus 15, the "Song of the Sea") and uses these images in a new context in order to proclaim God's intention that the exiles in Babylon will once again march in freedom to Zion:

Isaiah 51:9-11: Awake, awake, put on strength, O arm of the LORD! Awake, as in days of old, the generations of long ago! Was it not you who cut Rahab in pieces, who pierced the dragon? Was it not you who dried up the sea, the waters of the great deep; who made the depths of the sea a way for the redeemed to cross over? So the ransomed of the LORD shall return, and come to Zion with singing; everlasting joy shall be upon their heads; they shall obtain joy and gladness, and sorrow and sighing shall flee away.

Proverbs beautifully portrays God as creating in joy. Still the storm and sky images are contrasted with the sea images (note that the "sea" must be controlled, limited, but there is no battle). Creation is a joyful act of God (here narrated by personified Wisdom who watched the creation process):

Proverbs 8:27-31: When he established the heavens, I was there, when he drew a circle on the face of the deep, when he made firm the skies above, when he established the fountains of the deep, when he assigned to the sea its limit, so that the waters might not transgress his command, when he marked out the foundations of the earth, then I was beside him, like a master worker; and I was daily his delight, rejoicing before him always, rejoicing in his inhabited world and delighting in the human race.

Other scholars have argued that the version of the Creation Myth that the Hebrews would eventually come to know best was precisely the Babylonian version (Enuma Elish), because of their decades under Babylonian domination and as prisoners of war in the Babylonian heartland.

The point is simply this: the Hebrews knew the Combat Myth of their neighbors very well indeed. They referred to these myths, contrasted their beliefs against them, and even used the imagery in their poetry when it suited them. So why use the Combat Myth in the Genesis portrayal of creation? It is hard to avoid the conclusion that the peacefulness of the creation in Genesis 1 is entirely intentional, that the writer wanted us to know that God created *in peace,* and created *for peace.* Peacefulness, not conflict, is the order of the cosmos. The possibility of peace among humans (a part of God's creation) thus becomes far more real.

ADAM AND EVE: HUMAN CHALLENGES TO GOD'S PEACE

Once we read Genesis 1 in this powerful light—that God's creation was peaceful and intentional, and that humanity was created for peace—then we can better understand the second set of stories of Genesis that go further to explore the human violation of God's peace. By placing the seven-day story at the beginning, we then read the first sinful acts in Genesis 2–4 as a series of violent revolts against God's original, peaceful creation. The story progresses from the betrayal of trust between husband and wife to violence and murder between brothers to the final descent of all humanity into violence, leading God to regret having created us in the first place.

> **Genesis 6:5-6:** The LORD saw that the wickedness of humankind was great in the earth, and that every inclination of the thoughts of their hearts was only evil continually. And the LORD was sorry that he had made humankind on the earth, and it grieved him to his heart.

The point of this, of course, is that humanity was betraying God's peaceful intention:

> **Genesis 6:11-13:** Now the earth was corrupt in God's sight, and the earth was filled with violence. And God saw that the earth was corrupt; for all flesh had corrupted its ways upon the earth. And God said to Noah, "I have determined to make an end of all flesh, for the earth is filled with violence because of them; now I am going to destroy them along with the earth."

If humanity was naturally evil or naturally violent—then God would hardly be disappointed. It is precisely a series of violent acts that builds up to the flood accounts where God effectively starts over. Furthermore, lest we quickly try to explain that humanity may not have been originally violent but became naturally violent after the fall of Adam, let us quickly recall that Genesis portrays God's disappointment with human violence *after* Adam—after the fall when it was supposedly part of human nature. God was not content to merely sigh and say, "Oh well, fallen humans will be fallen humans" and sit back and watch the horrible show. Noah is the new start for humanity. It is perhaps not an accident that the first human experiment is erased by a flood—that is, by the enemy sea. So-called "natural violence" is rejected.

Some scholars speak of Genesis "building up" a series of sins to justify the flood. There is something of that here, but there is a bigger picture as well. If we take the book of Genesis as a whole, it now presents an interesting series of opening and closing thoughts. If the opening thoughts are: "God's peaceful intentions violated by human violence," then it is arguably the case that Genesis eventually leads to the idea that God's peaceful intentions are eventually, if not always consistently, embodied by human reconciliation.

What I mean is this: we spend so much time on the opening violence of humanity in Genesis that we often miss the striking examples of peacemaking implied in these narratives. Further, there are also significant conclusions in the Genesis tradition. In our previous discussion of Jacob and Esau, for example, we considered the stories as a tradition of peacemaking. Likewise the book of Genesis finishes, in the story of Joseph, with a profound act of forgiveness and a message of reconciliation.

JOSEPH AND HIS BROTHERS: "GOD SENT ME BEFORE YOU TO PRESERVE LIFE!"

It is common for readers of Genesis to presume that Joseph (at least after he began his travails in Egypt) was a kind and wise man who, through his endurance and insight, rose to prominence in the court of the Pharaoh. I think, however, that too many of us have given Joseph a bit too much benefit of the doubt. I think a careful reading of the relationship between Joseph and his brothers after Joseph's rise to prominence in Egypt reveals some important tensions in the story.

Joseph's trip to Egypt, of course, was the direct result of his brothers' jealousy and violence, and although he was spared from outright murder, he ended up being sold into slavery. The book of Genesis suggests that Joseph was a model of wisdom in Egypt and soon proved his worth to the elite of Egypt. Despite some dangerous threats, Joseph rose in the administration of the entire land. It is when he exercises considerable power, according to the tradition, that Joseph unexpectedly confronts his brothers. Joseph's Judean family has experienced famine, which is why the elder father Jacob sent his many sons into Egypt.

Egypt, we know, was frequently a place of refuge in times of famine because the Nile depends on waters from the rainforests of middle Africa and is usually not at the mercy of the same weather patterns as North Africa and Palestine. Thus, the Nile often provided irrigation water when other parts of the Middle East were in serious drought or famine.

The interaction between the powerful Joseph and his brothers begins in Genesis 42 and continues through the resolution of their relationship in chapter 45. The text clearly establishes Joseph's authority, but there is no hint that Joseph in his position of authority is somehow playing games in a friendly manner. Indeed, a straight reading of the text establishes Joseph's anger, even referring to the former events of his slavery:

> **Genesis 42:6-9:** Now Joseph was governor over the land; it was he who sold to all the people of the land. And Joseph's brothers came and bowed themselves before him with their faces to the ground. When Joseph saw his brothers, he recognized them, but he treated them like strangers and spoke harshly to them. "Where do you come from?" he said. They said, "From the land of Canaan, to buy food." Although Joseph had recognized his brothers, they did not recognize him. Joseph also remembered the dreams that he had dreamed about them. He said to them, "You are spies; you have come to see the nakedness of the land!"

The narrator presents the brothers rehearsing their behavior toward Joseph amongst themselves in their native language, not realizing that the Egyptian official standing over them is their brother Joseph, who understands everything they are saying. The unfolding of the events through conversation between the brothers, and eventually with the elder father Jacob/Israel, allows us to see the repentance of the brothers—but not yet of Joseph.

There is very little basis for the common idea that Joseph hatched this entire plan *intending all along* to reconcile with his brothers. A much more powerful reading of the story is that Joseph believes that this is his opportunity to have his revenge. There is an interesting parallel between the elaborate plan he is hatching and the elaborate dreams of the years of plenty and famine in Egypt that led to his rise in power in the first place. Both show the work of a calculating mind. I would argue, however, that the true turning point is highlighted in the Joseph story precisely when the elder brothers are one more time confronted by the Egyptian officials because of the apparent crime of their youngest brother, Benjamin:

> **Genesis 44:18:** Then Judah stepped up to him and said, "O my lord, let your servant please speak a word in my lord's ears, and do not be angry with your servant; for you are like Pharaoh himself."

Judah explains why they cannot leave Benjamin, even if he is guilty of a crime. Judah offers himself instead:

> **Genesis 44:33:** "Now therefore, please let your servant remain as a slave to my lord in place of the boy; and let the boy go back with his brothers. For how can I go back to my father if the boy is not with me? I fear to see the suffering that would come upon my father."

This is the turning point. When Judah offers himself, the text states, Joseph's heart melts:

> **Genesis 45:1-5:** Then Joseph could no longer control himself before all those who stood by him, and he cried out, "Send everyone away from me." So no one stayed with him when Joseph

made himself known to his brothers. And he wept so loudly that the Egyptians heard it, and the household of Pharaoh heard it. Joseph said to his brothers, "I am Joseph. Is my father still alive?" But his brothers could not answer him, so dismayed were they at his presence. Then Joseph said to his brothers, "Come closer to me." And they came closer. He said, "I am your brother, Joseph, whom you sold into Egypt. And now do not be distressed, or angry with yourselves, because you sold me here; for God sent me before you to preserve life."

The final observation is this. The book of Genesis begins by establishing creation and human society in peace. The book then narrates a long sequence of human rejection of God's peace. What is significant, however, is that the book closes with significant indications of peacemaking, reconciliation, and forgiveness. After a long sequence of passages about the relationships between the brothers, there is one final scene of repentance and forgiveness in the very last chapter. The final scene is all the more significant because it seems to return to the notion of forgiveness yet again— even though we appear to have settled things previously in Genesis 45. The text repeats a scene of forgiveness yet again:

Genesis 50:15-20: Realizing that their father was dead, Joseph's brothers said, "What if Joseph still bears a grudge against us and pays us back in full for all the wrong that we did to him?" So they approached Joseph, saying, "Your father gave this instruction before he died, 'Say to Joseph: I beg you, forgive the crime of your brothers and the wrong they did in harming you.' Now therefore please forgive the crime of the servants of the God of your father." Joseph wept when they spoke to him. Then his brothers also wept, fell down before him, and said, "We are here as your slaves." But Joseph said to them, "Do not be afraid! Am I in the place of God? Even though you intended to do harm to me, God intended it for good, in order to preserve a numerous people, as he is doing today."

Claus Westermann makes the interesting observation that Joseph's actions not only preserved the Hebrews (in providing for Jacob/Israel's family in times of famine) but also Joseph's wisdom in understanding his dreams led to the survival of all Egypt.[6] Thus, God's originally created peaceful order is restored at the conclusion of the book—although there is clear foreshadowing of the next step of the Hebrew story—the Exodus events. Whatever violence may also be a part of the Genesis story—and there is considerable violence—must be judged according to the clear message at the beginning and the end of the book—that God's intention is a peaceful order of creation. Violence is always a violation of God's creative intentions, and it is often our attempts to establish separations and borders between ourselves that create this violence.

God as Creator leads to an emphasis on peacefulness. The other major part of biblical literature that emphasizes God as Creator is Wisdom literature—best represented in the books of Proverbs, Ecclesiastes, Sirach, and Wisdom of Solomon. Do we see similar themes of peacefulness in these forms of Wisdom literature as well? Indeed we do. One interesting way to approach the Wisdom literature is to begin with biblical stories that illustrate Hebrews actually living by wisdom. One of the most striking examples of this pattern is Daniel.

II. WISDOM AND NONVIOLENCE

Proverbs 20:3: It is honorable to refrain from strife, but every fool is quick to quarrel.

A very interesting form of biblical literature arose in the time after the Exile. It has been called by many names: Lifestyle for the Diaspora, Diaspora Hero Stories, The Jews in the Court of the Foreign King, and the like. The basic idea is clear—fascinating stories were told about "one of us" working for "them," and how it worked out. Significantly, however, the "others" are usually represented by a foreign emperor and his advisors. In the case of the stories of Daniel (chapters 1–6), Daniel even works for the conqueror of Jerusalem. There are many of these stories, and they each take a somewhat different approach to the same general idea—Daniel works in the Babylonian and then Persian administration; Tobit persists under Assyrian domination; Esther marries the Emperor of Persia; and Joseph rises into prominence in ancient Egypt.

In each case, the Jewish central character must face a severe test of his or her ability to remain true to his or her faith and stay alive. In each of the stories of Daniel, for example, death (and horrible death at that) is always a very real threat. There is no getting around the fact that each of the stories represents the Jew not only in foreign settings but also in highly dangerous ones.

Similar to Daniel is the story of Tobit. Like Daniel and his friends, Tobit also resists assimilation into the foreign culture (Tobit 1:10-11—"But I kept myself from eating the food of the Gentiles"). In Tobit, it is said that he secretly buries murdered Israelites in the dangerous days of Sennacherib (Tobit 1:16-20). The story of his blindness begins with yet another case of the murder of an Israelite (2:3). Like Daniel, Tobit engages in acts of civil disobedience of the ruling authorities when those laws potentially violate his faith. So here are two themes—cooperation and resistance—that are discussed in these stories. How far can Daniel, Tobit, Esther, and others go in cooperating with the larger powers, "the nations," and when must they disobey and resist?

It has recently been suggested strongly that the Daniel stories (and Tobit as well) represent stories that illustrate wisdom—how the wise person behaves in the face of the threat of "the nations." The threat is always obvious—there is no "soft pedaling" who Nebuchadnezzar is in the Daniel stories. The opening verses of the book clarify—he is indeed the conqueror of Jerusalem. But in each story, Daniel and his friends use their faith and their wisdom to not only survive but also thrive. Clearly, each of these stories suggests that there are strategies for survival in the violent world, even when you live in hostile circumstances.

What is particularly interesting about the Daniel stories, however, is the implication that Daniel can survive and also actually have a significant impact on foreigners. Is it possible that one's wise behavior can actually have a transforming impact on enemies? The stories of Daniel seem to suggest precisely this.

At the end of the story of Daniel and his friends who eat pure food rather than the king's rations, the king is deeply impressed with the four Hebrews, and they are appointed to positions of authority (Dan. 1:18-21). But things begin to change. At the end of Daniel's interpretation of Nebuchadnezzar's dream, Daniel is not only promoted, but the foreign King is portrayed as exclaiming:

> **Daniel 2:47:** Truly, your God is God of gods and Lord of kings and a revealer of mysteries, for you have been able to reveal this mystery!

The speeches get longer. At the end of chapter 3, after the three Hebrews have successfully survived the fiery furnace, Nebuchadnezzar not only promotes them, he is apparently even more impressed than before:

> **Daniel 3:28-29:** Nebuchadnezzar said, "Blessed be the God of Shadrach, Meshach, and Abednego, who has sent his angel and delivered his servants who trusted in him. They disobeyed the king's command and yielded up their bodies rather than serve and worship any god except their own God. Therefore I make a decree: Any people, nation, or language that utters blasphemy against the God of Shadrach, Meshach, and Abednego shall be torn limb from limb, and their houses laid in ruins; for there is no other god who is able to deliver in this way."

Chapter four is the last chapter where King Nebuchadnezzar is featured, and it takes yet another step further, writing as if Nebuchadnezzar is himself telling the story and starting with a significant praise to the God of the Hebrews:

> **Daniel 4:2–3:** The signs and wonders that the Most High God has worked for me I am pleased to recount. How great are his signs, how mighty his wonders! His kingdom is an everlasting kingdom, and his sovereignty is from generation to generation.

At the end of his experiences, Nebuchadnezzar, the enemy of Israel, is clearly transformed to one with deep appreciation for the God of the universe. Note that there is nothing here to suggest that the story portrays Nebuchadnezzar having "converted" (how he is portrayed in the story, of course, has nothing to do with the historical figure). These stories portray Nebuchadnezzar as a new friend to the Hebrews who recognizes God:

> **Daniel 4:34-35:** When that period was over, I, Nebuchadnezzar, lifted my eyes to heaven, and my reason returned to me. I blessed the Most High, and praised and honored the one who lives forever. For his sovereignty is an everlasting sovereignty, and his kingdom endures from generation to generation. All the inhabitants of the earth are accounted as nothing, and he does what he wills with the host of heaven and the inhabitants of the earth. There is no one who can stay his hand or say to him, "What are you doing?"

And at the end of the stories about his rule, it is interesting that Nebuchadnezzar recognizes that God is not only Creator, but is a God of justice:

> **Daniel 4:37:** Now I, Nebuchadnezzar, praise and extol and honor the King of heaven, for all his works are truth, and his ways are justice; and he is able to bring low those who walk in pride.

Finally, we note at the end of the story of Daniel in the lions' den that Darius also comes to recognize the majesty of God and decrees an end to persecution of the Jews:

> **Daniel 6:26-27:** I make a decree, that in all my royal dominion people should tremble and fear before the God of Daniel: For he is the living God, enduring forever. His kingdom shall never be destroyed, and his dominion has no end. He delivers and rescues, he works signs and wonders in heaven and on earth; for he has saved Daniel from the power of the lions.

There are two elements of these stories that are especially interesting. First, Daniel models a nonviolent ethic in relation to "the nations." He resists assimilation, exhibits his wisdom, and remains a Hebrew through all the threats he faces, all without engaging in violence or plots of violence against the Babylonians or Persians. He does not give in but neither does he engage in violence.

The second notable aspect of these stories, however, is that Daniel certainly has an impact on foreigners. The foreign powers recognize the sovereignty of the God of the Hebrews, and this results in a workable existence. It would be a mistake to downplay either the resistance of Daniel or the wise nonviolence of Daniel, and it would be an even greater mistake to miss the implication of these stories that Daniel's strong wisdom can actually have a transformative impact on the foreign ruler. This is the key to what the Daniel stories (and the Esther and Joseph stories) offer—hope for the transformation of enemies. This transformation need not necessarily mean conversion—but it most certainly ends the violent threats. Daniel, in other words, models the use of brains over brawn, cleverness over brute strength. In this, Daniel himself exemplifies what the Wisdom books arguably teach.

Did cleverness come to challenge the more militant virtues seen in the other biblical books? Daniel represents an alternative to violent Hebrew ethics of national preservation because Daniel is shown to exhibit the ethics of wisdom. In this sense, wisdom gives rise to a tradition of clever, strategic, and personal quietism. There is a clear relationship between Daniel's pious, wise behavior and some of the peaceful advice of the Wisdom traditions of the Bible. Let us note some of the ways in which the ideal that Daniel embodied was spelled out in ancient Hebrew Wisdom.[7]

THE TEACHINGS OF THE WISE ONE

The Wisdom books of the Bible frequently contrast brute violence with wise peacefulness and resourceful cleverness. The book of Proverbs opens with an interesting conversation between a parent and a young man. In this advice, the young man is warned that there are those who would entice him to do violence for the sake of the financial rewards. There is even the interesting suggestion that the fellow bandits will become like an "evil family," sharing in the money stolen together:

Proverbs 1:10-15: My child, if sinners entice you, do not consent. If they say, "Come with us, let us lie in wait for blood; let us wantonly ambush the innocent; like Sheol let us swallow them alive and whole, like those who go down to the Pit. We shall find all kinds of costly things; we shall fill our houses with booty. Throw in your lot among us; we will all have one purse"—my child, do not walk in their way, keep your foot from their paths.

In contrast to the warrior or the bandit, the ideal Hebrew "Wise One" is calm and self-restrained, as Proverbs 17:27 advises, "One who spares words is knowledgeable, one who is cool in spirit has understanding." The Wise One seeks to end conflict before it begins, as Proverbs 17:9 enjoins, "One who forgives an affront fosters friendship, but one who dwells on disputes will alienate a friend," and note also 17:14, "The beginning of strife is like letting out water, so stop before the quarrel breaks out" (cf. 25:8-10, which advises that one settle matters out of court, which sounds a great deal like Matthew 25).

The Wise One will not return evil for evil, but seeks the welfare even of enemies. Proverbs 17:13 suggests, "Evil will not depart from the house of one who returns evil for good," and Proverbs 24:29 repeats the thought more directly by demanding that the Wise One must *not* say, "I will do to others as they have done to me; I will pay them back for what they have done."

Particularly when contrasted with militant Hellenistic virtues of the gallant hero-warrior, the Wise One appears quite different. Even in his apparent weakness, the Wise One is nevertheless protected by God (Prov. 2:7: "He stores up wisdom for the upright, He is a shield to those who walk blamelessly"; Prov. 16:7: "When the ways of people please the LORD, He causes even their enemies to be at peace with them"; Prov. 18:10-11: "The name of the LORD is a strong tower, the righteous run into it and are safe. The wealth of the rich is their strong city, in their imagination it is like a high wall").

It is particularly interesting how often this wisdom is contrasted with the fortifications of a town, such as Proverbs 16:32: "One who is slow to anger is better than the mighty and one whose

temper is controlled than one who captures a city."[8] The key here
is the contrast between the ways of the strong warrior and the
self-control, the restraint, and, indeed, peacefulness, of the wise.
This is particularly evident in Proverbs 21:22: "One wise person
went up against a city of warriors and brought down the strong-
hold in which they trusted." On reflection, it seems clear that we
are not intended to imagine a Samson-like conquest of an entire
city by brute strength, since it is precisely militant power that is
being contrasted with wisdom (perhaps we are to think of the
power of wisdom, as noted in Prov. 25:15: "With patience a ruler
may be persuaded and a soft tongue can break bones"). Compare
this with Proverbs 25:28: "Like a city breached, without walls, is
one who lacks self-control," which also, in a similar fashion, contrasts apparent strength with the strength of wisdom.

The theme of the one wise person against military strength is
also reflected elsewhere in Wisdom literature. This can be further
illustrated on the basis of the well-known passage in another
Wisdom book:

> **Ecclesiastes 9:13-18a:** I have also seen this example of wisdom
> under the sun, and it seemed great to me. There was a little city
> with few people in it. A great king came against it and besieged it,
> building great siegeworks against it. Now there was found in it a
> poor wise man, and he by his wisdom delivered the city. Yet no
> one remembered that poor man. So I said, "Wisdom is better than
> might; yet the poor man's wisdom is despised, and his words are
> not heeded." The quiet words of the wise are more to be heeded
> than the shouting of a ruler among fools. Wisdom is better than
> weapons of war.

How can these images of the single person against warriors
make any sense? This raises interesting questions about the interpretation of Proverbs 24:5-6:

> Wise warriors are mightier than strong ones and those who have
> knowledge than those who have strength; for by wise guidance
> you can wage your war, and in abundance of counselors there is
> victory.

Daniel embodies precisely this ethic of the Wise One, and it is hard not to notice the striking similarities between many of the themes of the stories of Daniel and the following pieces of advice in Wisdom books like Proverbs. Take, for example, the warning to be careful of the king's anger:

> **Proverbs 20:2:** The dread anger of a king is like the growling of a lion; anyone who provokes him to anger forfeits life itself.

Further, Daniel 1 may draw on advice such as the following:

> **Proverbs 23:3:** Do not desire the ruler's delicacies, for they are deceptive food.

Finally, Daniel's persona seems to embody the following:

> **Proverbs 25:5:** Take away the wicked from the presence of the king, and his throne will be established in righteousness. Do not put yourself forward in the king's presence or stand in the place of the great; for it is better to be told, "Come up here," than to be put lower in the presence of a noble.

I think we are justified in reading the Daniel stories as examples of Hebrew wisdom. Furthermore, Daniel's wise nonviolence is portrayed as having a positive impact on foreigners, who were transformed in the process. It remains to point out that this idea of having a positive and transforming impact on "the nations" is itself a deeply significant theme found mainly in the prophets.

We can summarize our survey of wisdom peacefulness and Daniel as an example in this way: war is about forcing changes. Defenders of war talk about "just wars." This means that the changes are thought to be necessary for justice. More often, however, these violent changes are simply desired by the more powerful party for their own interests (e.g., "our national interest"). Wisdom literature suggests that positive changes can be accomplished without violence. There is a Gandhian practicality to Wisdom literature's praise of thought over strength—a thoughtful process that can lead to change where change is just and necessary.

THE INTERNATIONAL NEGOTIATIONS FOR PEACE ON MOUNT ZION, OR: HOW TO BEAT WEAPONS INTO FARMING TOOLS

Scholars often point to the numerous prophetic passages that picture the nations' march into Jerusalem (usually described as Zion) because they have come to recognize God. Is there a connection between Daniel's proposed influence on the enemy and some of these passages that speak of a new era when the nations will march to Zion? I think that there is. But once again, we must contend with different voices in the biblical text on this issue.

Notice that some of these passages about the nations coming to Zion (they are usually called Procession of the Nations passages) are quite vindictive:

> **Isaiah 49:22-26:** Thus says the Lord GOD: I will soon lift up my hand to the nations, and raise my signal to the peoples; and they shall bring your sons in their bosom, and your daughters shall be carried on their shoulders. Kings shall be your foster fathers, and their queens your nursing mothers. With their faces to the ground they shall bow down to you, and lick the dust of your feet. Then you will know that I am the LORD; those who wait for me shall not be put to shame. Can the prey be taken from the mighty, or the captives of a tyrant be rescued? But thus says the LORD: Even the captives of the mighty shall be taken, and the prey of the tyrant be rescued; for I will contend with those who contend with you, and I will save your children. I will make your oppressors eat their own flesh, and they shall be drunk with their own blood as with wine. Then all flesh shall know that I am the LORD your Savior, and your Redeemer, the Mighty One of Jacob.

In the following passage, "the nations" come to work and bring their resources to give to the Hebrew people. This portrays an empire being forced to bring taxes and payments, very much like the Persian and Hellenistic empires were often portrayed in their carvings:

Isaiah 60:10-12: Foreigners shall build up your walls, and their kings shall minister to you; for in my wrath I struck you down, but in my favor I have had mercy on you. Your gates shall always be open; day and night they shall not be shut, so that nations shall bring you their wealth, with their kings led in procession. For the nation and kingdom that will not serve you shall perish; those nations shall be utterly laid waste.

In both of these portrayals of the Procession, the march is described as virtually a conquest—as if the nations have no choice.

But there is another tradition—a different voice—that presents the nations as actually learning something and then seeking to know more:

Zechariah 8:20-23: Thus says the LORD of hosts: Peoples shall yet come, the inhabitants of many cities; the inhabitants of one city shall go to another, saying, "Come, let us go to entreat the favor of the LORD, and to seek the LORD of hosts; I myself am going." Many peoples and strong nations shall come to seek the LORD of hosts in Jerusalem, and to entreat the favor of the LORD. Thus says the LORD of hosts: In those days ten men from nations of every language shall take hold of a Jew, grasping his garment and saying, "Let us go with you, for we have heard that God is with you."

The most recognized of this theme of "the nations" choosing to learn peace, of course, is also the most well-known peace passage in the entire Bible. But notice the role of teaching and learning in this passage:

Isaiah 2:2-5: In days to come the mountain of the LORD's house shall be established as the highest of the mountains, and shall be raised above the hills; all the nations shall stream to it. Many peoples shall come and say, "Come, let us go up to the mountain of the LORD, to the house of the God of Jacob; that he may teach us his ways and that we may walk in his paths." For out of Zion shall go forth instruction, and the word of the LORD from Jerusalem. He shall judge between the nations, and shall arbitrate for many peoples; they shall beat their swords into plowshares, and their spears into pruning hooks; nation shall not lift up sword against nation, neither shall they learn war any more. O house of Jacob, come, let us walk in the light of the LORD!

Clearly, not all of the procession themes portray the nations being forced and conquered. When the nations learn, according to Isaiah 2 (and the parallel passage in Micah 4), the consequence is that wars cease. This is all the more striking in the context of Nebuchadnezzar's exclamation that he has learned something about God: "For all his works are truth, and his ways are justice."

CONCLUSION

Among the more surprising of the teachings of Jesus in the Gospel of Matthew is one that I am particularly fond of: "I am sending you out like sheep into the midst of wolves; so be wise as serpents and innocent as doves" (Matt. 10:16). The people of God are the sheep—it is a positive image. Sheep-like people are trusting, and perhaps a bit defenseless if they are not warned. Wolves, on the other hand, are dangerous and unpredictable. Listening to Jesus, we might have expected a second contrast to go with the first contrast between animals:

Sheep GOOD and Wolves BAD,

so one would have expected, similarly:

Doves GOOD and Serpents BAD.

But here is the surprising twist in Jesus' saying. Like the contrast between Sheep and Wolf, we expect "Be like doves, not like serpents." But Jesus startles us—as if to say in so many words, "Don't be naive." To be innocent as doves means that you must also be as wise as serpents. Therefore, to be sent as sheep, we are armed with wisdom. I propose that Jesus' short zoological lesson (learning from animal observation is a common wisdom theme) contains within it the seeds of one of the basic paradoxes of Christian life—our relationship to the world and society around us. The Gospel of John features Jesus warning us of the wolves in even stronger terms. It is John's Gospel in the fifteenth chapter, for example, that carefully recalls Jesus saying, "Don't be surprised if the world hates you." Paul will later echo his Messiah by speaking of the "principalities and powers of this world" against which we are in opposition. There is caution here, a warning to maintain your guard. And this is a powerful and important theme. Christians must never underestimate the opposition. Nonconformity to the world is a lifestyle that Christian faith calls forth in relation to the world, and it is never to be engaged in without thought. We are to be armed by wisdom literally. See how the passage in Wisdom of Solomon 5:16-20 becomes, in Paul's hands, the more profound nonviolent idea in Ephesians 6:10-17.

This is not a mere turn of phrase. To be wise is to be armed for a kind of battle. When we consider Daniel 11:32-33, undoubtedly written in a later age than the stories of Daniel 1–6, we nevertheless see the theme of wisdom in a most interesting manner. Listen to the praise of the faithful when it is written that in the midst of persecutions and trials:

> **Daniel 11:32-33:** The people who are loyal to their God shall stand firm and take action. The wise among the people shall give understanding to many.

Here you have the call to do battle, but the weapon is to teach the truth. Peter sounds the call. In 1 Peter 1:13, the old call to prepare for battle is cited: "Gird up your loins"; but the image he combines with this is striking—"Prepare your minds for action." Discipline yourself and set your hope not in swords, lances, soldiers, armies, or missiles, but in the grace of Jesus Christ. Along these lines, Daniel 11:32-33 seems parallel to 1 Peter 1:13.

The revolutionary acts of Hebrew coyotes in violating human borders for peace and justice are not acts of violence, but engagements in teaching—sometimes directly, sometimes by example—and it will involve crossing dangerous borders. It is the wise action of a Daniel, however, that may well attract many in "the nations" to reconsider the false wisdom of their old ways of violence and injustice.

It goes without saying (almost) that we can hardly ask others for peace and nonviolence, however, if we haven't already committed ourselves to be harmless as doves.

Chapter Six

Jesus Violates the Borders

F inally, we arrive at the greatest border runner of them all—the one whom Matthew writes up as "the new Moses." (Moses, of course, being a border runner of no mean accomplishment himself.)

JESUS AS THE GOOD COYOTE

There is little debate that Jesus, as portrayed in the mature Gospels of Matthew and Luke especially, is a Messiah who will have direct relationships to Gentiles. Both Gospels portray the very origins of the mission of Jesus, as well as God's affirmation of Jesus as the Son of God, in the context of the famous Isaiah 49:6 concept of "bringing light to the nations":

> **Matthew 12:15b-21:** Many crowds followed him, and he cured all of them, and he ordered them not to make him known. This was to fulfill what had been spoken through the prophet Isaiah: "Here is my servant, whom I have chosen, my beloved, with whom my soul is well pleased. I will put my Spirit upon him, and he will proclaim justice to the Gentiles. He will not wrangle or cry aloud, nor will anyone hear his voice in the streets. He will not break a bruised reed or quench a smoldering wick until he brings justice to victory. And in his name the Gentiles will hope."

When the child Jesus is presented to an elder named Simeon, his reply is taken as significant in understanding the mission of Jesus:

> **Luke 2:29-32:** Master, now you are dismissing your servant in peace, according to your word; for my eyes have seen your salvation, which you have prepared in the presence of all peoples, a light for revelation to the Gentiles and for glory to your people Israel.

The border crossing theme is obvious in Luke. To read, in this context, Jesus' own declaration of his intentions to bring a word of liberation to the Gentiles as well as the Jews in Luke 4 is too easy. In this chapter, however, I want to argue that Matthew's "new Moses" portrayal of Jesus is just as revolutionary in its advocacy of border running.

In the light of the Hebrew precedents, one can argue that the writer of Matthew sees the major theme of the peacefulness of Jesus as directly connected to the repentence of "the nations"—the turning of foreigners to see the truth. Consider the interesting comment made by Jesus:

> **Matthew 11:21:** Woe to you, Chorazin! Woe to you, Bethsaida! For if the deeds of power done in you had been done in Tyre and Sidon, they would have repented long ago in sackcloth and ashes.

Tyre and Sidon, of course, are outside the realm of Judean territory, where Elijah traveled to visit the Syro-Phoenician woman (1 Kings 17), and are referred to in the Bible as nearby territories famous for their maritime trade. But the reference to sackcloth and ashes seems a direct reference to Jonah, since it is the only occasion in the later Hebrew texts (it doesn't appear in older texts) where a foreign people take on these symbols of repentance (Jon. 3:6, but of Hebrews see: Esth. 4:1, 3; Isa. 58:5; Jer. 6:26; Dan. 9:3), and it is referred to in other sayings of Jesus about the "sign of Jonah" (Luke 11:29-30).

This is precisely the connection that I want to make in a brief survey of key Matthean passages—namely that the peacefulness and nonviolence of Jesus is directly related to his standing in the tradition of Hebrew coyotes who violate borders for the sake of peace. Furthermore, as many New Testament scholars now affirm, Jesus must be read in the context of Roman-occupied Palestine.

How do we understand the peaceful teachings of Jesus today? The typical consensus about Jesus remains something like this: he may have taught some kind of peacefulness, but this quiet ethic was, and remains, not very practical in the real world. Others might add that the peaceful teaching of Jesus was a peacefulness that could hardly be called nonviolent, given the violence of the Hebrew tradition in which he stood. Still others cite episodes like the cleansing of the Temple as an indication that Jesus himself may not have been so peaceful all the time.

In general, the nonviolence of Jesus is usually challenged on three counts: (1) There was no Hebrew precedent for nonviolence; (2) Jesus did not even mean to teach what we call nonviolence in his own time because we are reading our modern notions into the first century; and (3) Christianity, therefore, did not adopt a nonviolent ethic because Jesus did not really provide one. I propose to answer each of these.

I have thus far mounted a challenge to the first argument, citing significant Hebrew precedents for precisely a biblical Hebrew ethic of nonviolence within the context of "crossing borders." I have already cited the roughly contemporary example of Rabbi Yochanon ben Zakkai to challenge the second argument by citing at least one first-century example of Hebrew quietism and even antiwar ethics, and I will now turn to further elements of challenging the second argument. Then, I will begin a discussion in response to the third argument by briefly discussing aspects of the final book of the New Testament, the Apocalypse of John, to argue for a nonviolence of early Christianity.

"LOVE YOUR ENEMIES" AND ROMAN IMPERIALISM

In the previous chapters, I have argued that the Babylonian occupation and, finally, the destruction of Jerusalem, were key events from which to understand the emergent debates in ancient Israel about the relationship between the Jews and the nations/the others. This event needs to remain at the center of any reading context for most of the Hebrew Bible/Old Testament.

It is interesting, then, to point out that in recent New Testament scholarship, scholars like Richard Horsley, Klaus Wengst, and Bruce Malina (among many others) have all contributed important work insisting that a very similar violent imperial context of Roman-occupied Palestine must be the backdrop to any understanding of the teachings of Jesus.[1] Furthermore, at least John, Luke, and Matthew reflect aspects of the Roman conquest of Jerusalem in 70 CE as well (Mark may be earlier). As Richard Horsley writes:

> Jesus pursued his mission in a historical period framed by imperial violence against the Judean and Galilean people and their repeated struggle for independence. Imperial violence was perhaps the most important broadly determinative factor in the circumstances of his mission and the movement that he catalyzed.[2]

How does this impact our understanding of specific teachings of Jesus? Horsley argues that in his message, Jesus called for a new unity among the Jewish people and especially directed his message to those disenfranchised Jews—the poor and the neglected—who were suffering the most from economic occupation and imposition of Roman material and legal structures on the occupied Jewish populations. In this context, then, Horsley wants to argue that a teaching like "Love your enemies" is, in fact, part of Jesus' call to Jewish communities that are disintegrating under the crushing rule of Roman occupation. In this reading, Jesus intended to shore up Jewish communal solidarity and especially calls on his fellow Jews to stop taking their anger out on each other. The enemies that Jesus was referring to, then, were fellow Jews, according to Horsley. He takes this interesting argument even further with regard to other teachings of Jesus: The one to whom you must "lend freely," for example, was a fellow Jew in difficult circumstances of occupation.

In his longer defense of a new reading for the teachings of Jesus, Horsley argues that the message of Jesus could be summarized by the following statement: "Take responsibility for willingly helping one another, even your enemies, in the local Jewish community."[3]

Does this make sense? Have we misunderstood Jesus when he said "Love your enemies"? Have we mistakenly read Jesus to be referring to the Romans and other foreigners as "enemies" when he really meant, so to speak, "love your fellow Jews that you aren't getting along with like you should"? If so, then one major aspect of the "border running" teachings of Jesus would need to be reexamined. But does this argument hold up on examination? On this issue, I will disagree with my friend, whose work I admire, but because Horsley's interesting argument bears directly on our presentation of Jesus as a nonviolent "border runner," I would like to consider some further details of this fascinating argument more carefully by focusing on Jesus' teaching in Matthew especially and in the context of the tradition of Hebrew coyotes who came before him. Although I will try to keep this argument fairly brief in the paragraphs that follow, there are some important details to keep in mind. The importance of the details, however, will hopefully be clear to all, especially a review of the importance of the "Q" source.

"LOVE YOUR ENEMIES . . ." IN THE CONTEXT OF THE ROMAN CENTURION

Among the more interesting aspects of scholarly research on the Gospels has been the sophisticated development of the reading of earlier "layers" of the sayings of Jesus within the Gospels as we now have them. Claiming that anything is a "virtual consensus" in Biblical Studies is asking for trouble, I realize, but by now, a virtual consensus does seem to exist such that Matthew and Luke used older sources. Among these sources is the older Gospel of Mark, and also a common collection of the sayings of Jesus called "Q" (for *Quelle*, or Source). This hardly comes as a big surprise in the case of Luke, particularly since the writer clearly tells us at the beginning of his Gospel that previous accounts of the life and teachings of Jesus already exist, and he simply wants to improve upon them (Luke 1:1-4).

Where these insights about layers of the traditions of the teachings of Jesus become more controversial is when scholars argue that we can therefore get "behind" the Gospel of Luke and the Gospel of Matthew and not only identify the older sayings of Jesus that they used but also comment on what they may have originally meant *before* Matthew or Luke placed them in their present contexts in the two Gospels. Of course, we already know that these two Gospels do use some of the sayings of Jesus in a somewhat different way. This is immediately obvious from the fact that Matthew—following his tendency to read the events of the life and ministry of Jesus in line with the events of the life of Moses—locates Jesus on the Mount (like Moses on Sinai) when Matthew presents a central series of the teachings of Jesus (e.g., "Sermon on the Mount"). Luke, on the other hand, places him "on a level place" (Luke 6:17) to say many of the same things (but not in exactly the same words—thus the so-called "Sermon on the Plain"). This isn't a huge issue, of course, but it does illustrate that there is some freedom that the Gospel writers have in using their sources. Does this also suggest that the Gospel writers actually changed the significance of some of the sayings of Jesus? If so, can we identify what these words originally meant before Matthew or Luke used them? Some New Testament scholars think we can by identifying how these teachings read in their "older context" in the "Q" source.

The portion of "Q" that we are interested in appears together with other sayings in a collection, or series, of sayings of Jesus that amount to lessons for life. This series reads like a collection of wise sayings in the tradition of a Hebrew book like Proverbs or even Ecclesiastes, and it would, therefore, not surprise us to notice that it is in this collection of sayings where some of Jesus' most direct notions of nonviolence appear since we have already noted that there is so much praise for peacefulness and restraint in wisdom traditions. Perhaps "Q" was something like "The Wisdom of Jesus" in its original conception? In any case, using the numbering system from the way the sayings appear in the Gospel of Luke, it has been proposed that the following series of teachings is how the original "Q" source read before Luke and Matthew placed them in their Gospels:

> **6:20:** And raising his eyes to his disciples he said: Blessed are you poor, for God's reign is for you.

> **6:21:** Blessed are you who hunger for you will eat your fill. Blessed are you who mourn for you will be consoled.

> **6:22:** Blessed are you when they insult and persecute you, and say every kind of evil against you because of the son of humanity.

> **6:23:** Be glad and exult, for vast is your reward in heaven. For this is how they persecuted the prophets who were before you.

There is some controversy here as to whether the following three verses actually appeared in "Q":

> **Luke 6:24-26:** But woe to you who are rich, for you have received your consolation. Woe to you who are full now, for you will be hungry. Woe to you who are laughing now, for you will mourn and weep. Woe to you when all speak well of you, for that is what their ancestors did to the false prophets.

The reconstruction, however, normally continues with the following:

> **6:27:** Love your enemies

> **6:28:** and pray for those persecuting you

> **6:35c-d:** so that you may become sons of your Father, for he raises his sun on bad and good and rains on the just and unjust.

> **6:29:** The one who slaps you on the cheek, offer him the other as well; and to the person wanting to take you to court and get your shirt, turn over to him the coat as well.

> **6:29-30/Matt 5:41:** And the one who conscripts you for one mile, go with him a second.

6:30: To the one who asks of you, give; and from the one who borrows, do not ask back what is yours.

6:31: And the way you want people to treat you, that is how you treat them.

6:32: If you love those loving you, what reward do you have? Do not even tax collectors do the same?

6:34: And if you lend to those from whom you hope to receive, what reward do you have? Do not even the Gentiles to the same?

6:41: And why do you see the speck in your brother's eye, but the beam in your own eye you overlook?

6:42: How can you say to your brother: Let me throw out the speck from your eye, and just look at the beam in your own eye? Hypocrite, first throw out from your own eye the beam, and then you will see clearly to throw out the speck in your brother's eye.

The section finishes (6:47-49) with Jesus' analogy that obeying his sayings is like building your house on a rock rather than sand. This most certainly does borrow from a famous Hebrew wisdom teaching technique, the comparison between the wise man and the foolish man, which is common in Proverbs (Prov. 10:8, 14, 23, etc.).

The point is, "Love your enemies" would appear to be one of the most unequivocal statements of "crossing borders" for peace in the entire Bible. But is it? Since Gentiles are negatively cited in 6:34, similar to tax collectors in 6:32, some have argued that the love command does not really apply to national enemies like Romans (Gentiles) but rather to fellow Hebrews. In this argument, Jesus is not advocating a different treatment of Roman occupiers as opposed to the other Jewish resisters who use violence to resist Roman occupation. The claim is, then, that Jesus was not teaching nonviolence against those who engaged in violence because he was simply not talking about the Romans or other Gentiles. In reply, I would make a number of observations.

Now, it is widely argued that the "go the second mile" passage as well as the "strike on the cheek" passage both seem to be an integral part of this original series of the teachings of Jesus. Both are arguably clear references to life under Roman occupation— being struck with the back of the hand (compare the striking of Jesus in the passion accounts) and a reference to any Roman soldier's right to demand that any non-Roman may be asked to bear the soldier's pack for one mile if the soldier wants assistance. So, foreign "enemies" are cited not far from Jesus' command to "love your enemy."[4]

Can "love your enemies" really be so easily separated from "go the extra mile," which obviously does apply to Roman occupation forces, as Walter Wink has effectively argued?[5] I would go further, however. We have seen how Hebrew coyotes, writing of processions of nations, actually imply that Gentiles will regret their violence before God. Did this Old Testament theme also inspire Matthew's reflections on Jesus' own interactions with a specific Roman soldier?

Already in the "Q" reconstruction suggested above, these sayings are accompanied by the story of the healing of the centurion's servant. Critical reproductions of "Q" generally agree that this episode of healing the centurion's son should be included in "Q" material, which appears in Matthew in chapter 8, immediately following the conclusion of the sermon:

> **Matthew 8:5-13:** When he entered Capernaum, a centurion came to him, appealing to him and saying, "Lord, my servant is lying at home paralyzed, in terrible distress." And he said to him, "I will come and cure him." The centurion answered, "Lord, I am not worthy to have you come under my roof; but only speak the word, and my servant will be healed. For I also am a man under authority, with soldiers under me; and I say to one, 'Go,' and he goes, and to another, 'Come,' and he comes, and to my slave, 'Do this,' and the slave does it." When Jesus heard him, he was amazed and said to those who followed him, "Truly I tell you, in no one in Israel have I found such faith. I tell you, many will come from east and west and will eat with Abraham and Isaac and Jacob in the king-

dom of heaven, while the heirs of the kingdom will be thrown into the outer darkness, where there will be weeping and gnashing of teeth." And to the centurion Jesus said, "Go; let it be done for you according to your faith." And the servant was healed in that hour.

Here is where the argument becomes especially difficult—because some scholars argue that the "Centurion's Son" episode is a secondary addition inspired by later concerns for the Gentile mission. This is, however, an interesting "chicken and egg" problem. Couldn't the fully engaged Gentile missions of the first generation of Christians have been inspired by such specific actions of Jesus? Still, some want to argue that the oldest sayings of Jesus talked about "Love your enemies" but without referring to any Romans or Gentiles; then another layer of "Q" added the healing of the Roman centurion, then an even later editor composing Matthew added the other healings surrounding the centurion, as chapter 8 of Matthew now reads. It begins to sound complicated, especially if we do have Hebrew precedent for Jesus' own views and actions.

The conclusion is then reached, based on this kind of multilayered reading, that Jesus did not originally intend to extend "love of enemies" to the Gentiles—but that a later "Q" editor and then the writer of Matthew yet again both added material about Gentiles (perhaps under the influence of later Christian idealism inspired by Paul's Gentile mission?), which then strongly influenced how we understand "enemies" in the saying of Jesus. The alleged additions changed the meaning of "enemies" to include foreigners. Does this make sense? More to the point—are there historical or biblical grounds for the idea that Jesus could have actually taught positively about Gentiles?

Few readers would dispute that the Gospel of Matthew as we now have it (and certainly also the Gospel of Luke) most certainly *does* understand Jesus' commandments to apply to Gentiles. But that was not, some would argue, Jesus' *original i*ntention. Originally, Jesus was speaking only of fellow Hebrews—trying to repair local Hebrew solidarity in their struggle against the ravages of Roman occupation. At this point, I have to ask whether this intriguing argument is fully alive to the various prophetic traditions that we have already argued are central to war and peace, violence and nonviolence questions in the Hebrew tradition. In other words, I would argue that the nonviolence of Jesus cannot be assessed apart from *the radical inclusivity of Jesus, because the nonviolence of Jesus partially derives from his application (and indeed, fulfillment) of the Hebrew precedents which we have been exploring in the Hebrew scriptures.*

Let us explore further examples of Jesus' inclusive attitudes to foreigners as illustrated by certain selected texts. The collective reading of all these texts, especially in the context of the Hebrew precedents we have already examined, leads me to the view that Jesus actually stands at the very center of that Hebrew coyote tradition that soundly criticized the one-sided, destructive hatred of the nations that we see in *some parts* of the Hebrew biblical tradition. Let us begin by finishing our analysis of the story of the centurion.

I. Jesus and the Roman Centurion—Is Jesus Illustrating Jonah?

In the "Q" version of the healing of the centurion, the centurion claims that he is not worthy (*ikonos*—competent, able; in the Greek Old Testament, it is the same term Moses uses to protest his "unworthiness" before the burning bush). But what makes him unworthy? He explains that he is a man with authority and that he commands others. In short, he is an occupying soldier. The issue appears to be his military authority. The centurion claims that he is not worthy precisely *because* he has this power or authority (*exousia*). The term used here is often used of political power in late pre-Christian Jewish texts, specifically the powerful authority of foreign rulers over Israel (in 1 Maccabees—authority to raise troops or taxes, 10:6, 8, 35). This term for power or authority can also be used figuratively—in Psalm 126:8, 9 the sun "rules" over the day, and moon and stars "rule" over the night; and Joseph was given "authority" over his former masters in Egypt by means of wisdom, personified as Lady Wisdom:

> **Wisdom 10:14:** And when he was in prison she did not leave him, until she brought him the scepter of a kingdom and authority over

his masters. Those who accused him she showed to be false, and she gave him everlasting honor.

But it is an especially important term used throughout the Greek translation of the book of Daniel, with its stories set in the context of Babylonian power over Hebrews (Dan. 5:16, 29; 6:3). And it was a term added heavily in the Theodotian Greek version of Daniel, such as in chapter 4 where Nebuchadnezzar's kingdom and authority will be given to another to rule.[6]

Perhaps the most intriguing passage that relates to our reading of a story of Jesus interacting with a centurion, is a passage from the book of Sirach which advises caution in *doing precisely what Jesus is described as doing in the Gospels*—that is, approaching those with such power/authority:

> **Sirach 9:13:** Keep far from those who have power/authority to kill, and you will not be haunted by the fear of death. But if you approach them, make no misstep, or they may rob you of your life. Know that you are stepping among snares, and that you are walking on the city battlements.

With all of this in mind, let us reflect on this scene for a moment. The Roman centurion approaches a member of the occupied peoples and then confesses that he is not worthy precisely because he is an occupying soldier. Are we seeing a New Testament illustration of "the nations" coming to Zion and "learning war no more" (Isa. 2:2-4)? When this episode is placed in the context of Jesus' own teaching about loving enemies, and also Jesus' frequent references to Jonah, it is hard to avoid the probability that the episode of Jesus interacting with a centurion is intended to precisely illustrate the repentance of the Gentiles— the transformation of the enemy. And, as we have seen, this is a clear Hebrew coyote tradition.

I think it would be a bit odd to suggest that a later writer, the Gospel writer of Matthew or Luke, was **more** aware of the Hebrew precedents that stand behind Jesus' attitude toward foreigners (what we are calling the tradition of the Hebrew coyotes) than Jesus himself would have been. I think it is a more logical argument that Jesus quite intentionally placed himself in this tradition of violating borders for peace and knew very well that his interaction with a Roman centurion was an illustration of his own teaching about loving enemies as well as, and in addition to, his references to Jonah.

Other passages would tend to support such a reading as well. If we read the centurion's confession before Jesus alongside a Markan passage that is also used by both Luke and Matthew, an interesting connection is suggested:

> **Mark 10:42:** So Jesus called them and said to them, "You know that among the Gentiles those whom they recognize as their rulers lord it over them, and their great ones are tyrants over them."

The term for "tyrants" is a compound Greek term that uses the same word for "authority" that the centurion used. Thus, this kind of "power/authority" is repudiated by the centurion (or, at the very least, is a source of great embarrassment for him) and is further repudiated by Jesus himself because this kind of leadership has no place among his disciples. It is precisely this kind of violent authority that Jesus denies to those who would be his followers. Instead, Christian leadership is servanthood:

> **Mark 10:43-45:** But it is not so among you; but whoever wishes to become great among you must be your servant, and whoever wishes to be first among you must be slave of all. For the Son of Man came not to be served but to serve, and to give his life a ransom for many.

Can our reading of these teachings of Jesus be supported with reading other important New Testament passages? I think it can.

II. The Cleansing of the Temple

We can cite another example in this brief survey of the "coyote teachings" of Jesus. All four Gospels portray the public demonstration of Jesus in the Temple—often called the cleansing of the

Temple. Readers are familiar with the events, but what I want to emphasize is the specific quotations by Jesus on each occasion. In particular, the phrase "den of robbers" has an important history. This phrase was borrowed from one of the series of sermons that are now part of the book of Jeremiah. But this is a particularly radical phrase, and it comes from a sermon of the prophet that is perhaps the most famous of Jeremiah's condemning sermons— the Temple Sermon, in which Jeremiah threatened the destruction of the Temple because of the hypocrisy of those who offered sacrifices there:

> **Jeremiah 7:9-11:** Will you steal, murder, commit adultery, swear falsely, make offerings to Baal, and go after other gods that you have not known, and then come and stand before me in this house, which is called by my name, and say, "We are safe!"— only to go on doing all these abominations? Has this house, which is called by my name, become a den of robbers in your sight? You know, I too am watching, says the LORD.

So Jesus quotes Jeremiah. The other part of the phrases cited by Jesus in the Temple is: "My father's house should be a house of prayer." This phrase is drawn from one of the most radically inclusive texts of the book of Isaiah. In this text, not only eunuchs (that is, those who have physical imperfections) but also foreigners, will not be rejected. It is significant to read the entire important passage:

> **Isaiah 56:1-8:** Thus says the LORD: Maintain justice, and do what is right, for soon my salvation will come, and my deliverance be revealed. Happy is the mortal who does this, the one who holds it fast, who keeps the sabbath, not profaning it, and refrains from doing any evil. Do not let the foreigner joined to the LORD say, "The LORD will surely separate me from his people," and do not let the eunuch say, "I am just a dry tree." For thus says the LORD: To the eunuchs who keep my sabbaths, who choose the things that please me and hold fast my covenant, I will give, in my house and within my walls, a monument and a name better than sons and daughters; I will give them an everlasting name that shall not be

cut off. And the foreigners who join themselves to the LORD, to minister to him, to love the name of the LORD, and to be his servants, all who keep the sabbath, and do not profane it, and hold fast my covenant—these I will bring to my holy mountain, and make them joyful in my house of prayer; their burnt offerings and their sacrifices will be accepted on my altar; for my house shall be called a house of prayer for all peoples. Thus says the Lord GOD, who gathers the outcasts of Israel, I will gather others to them besides those already gathered.

I argue that one of the main reasons that Jesus' action resulted in the lethal hostility of the Temple personnel on this occasion is because of the specific combination of these two passages. Jesus quoted from Jeremiah 7; this implies that Jesus believed that the Temple where he then stood was *also liable to the same destructive judgment* that Jeremiah threatened for the first Temple. However, by specifically combining this threat with Isaiah 56, the *further* implication for Jesus is that he believes that among the "sins" for which the Temple will be judged is precisely a *lack of inclusivity of "foreigners"*—one of the hallmarks of Jesus' own movement and message. In short, the social injustices that Jeremiah originally spoke of in referring to the "den of robbers" is amended by Jesus to now **include** not having an open attitude toward repentant foreigners. Jesus thus clarifies his open opposition to an exclusive attitude of maintaining borders when they need to be violated in the name of the kingdom of God.

III. THE SYRO-PHOENICIAN WOMAN

We can cite one final example to illustrate Jesus' radical border crossings in the tradition of the Gospel of Matthew (borrowed, perhaps, from Mark):

Matthew 15:21-28: Jesus left that place and went away to the district of Tyre and Sidon. Just then a Canaanite woman from that region came out and started shouting, "Have mercy on me, Lord, Son of David; my daughter is tormented by a demon." But he did not answer her at all. And his disciples came and urged him, saying, "Send her away, for she keeps shouting after us." He answered, "I was sent only to the lost sheep of the house of Israel." But she came and knelt before him, saying, "Lord, help me." He answered, "It is not fair to take the children's food and throw it to the dogs." She said, "Yes, Lord, yet even the dogs eat the crumbs that fall from their masters' table." Then Jesus answered her, "Woman, great is your faith! Let it be done for you as you wish." And her daughter was healed instantly.

There are many aspects of this story that commentators and readers of the New Testament have found both troubling and fascinating. It is normally noted, for example, that this episode follows (in Mark and Matthew) a lengthy series of dialogues by Jesus on violating normal Jewish purity regulations by declaring that it is what comes out of a person that makes them unclean, not what they eat (Matt. 7:10-11; Mark 7:17-23). The story of the dialogue with a Gentile woman, therefore, follows a logic about including people who were considered unclean even if this is against previous views of Jewish/Gentile relations.

Many readers seem troubled by the shortness, even nastiness, of the attitude of Jesus toward the woman. He is silent at first and then when he speaks, he compares her to dogs. As Joel Marcus points out in his extended discussion of this passage, it will not do to suggest that Jesus meant "puppy" and wasn't intending an insult.[7] The overwhelming evidence of the Hebrew Bible and early rabbinic tradition is that "dog" was a serious insult, and not unusual as a term for a Gentile (cf. 1 Sam. 17:43; Prov. 26:11; Sirach 26:25, "A headstrong wife is regarded as a *dog*, but one who has a sense of shame will fear the Lord"). The term can be used, however, of enemies as well (Ps. 22:16; 59:6), and in Jeremiah it appears in a suggestive series of prophetic judgments:

Jeremiah 15:2b-4: Thus says the LORD: Those destined for pestilence, to pestilence, and those destined for the sword, to the sword; those destined for famine, to famine, and those destined for captivity, to captivity. And I will appoint over them four kinds of destroyers, says the LORD: the sword to kill, the *dogs* to drag away, and the birds of the air and the wild animals of the earth to devour and destroy. I will make them a horror to all the kingdoms of the earth because of what King Manasseh son of Hezekiah of Judah did in Jerusalem.

What I think we can suggest is this: our attention in this passage is too often focused on the apparently "poor woman" who begs from Jesus. I believe, however, that the focus on her gender may thus overlook the central issue—she is a stranger, a Gentile. Many commentators wish to suggest that the woman is actually of some economic means. What I will suggest, however, is that the act of kneeling before Jesus is the critically important detail, although not often mentioned in the context of the Hebrew tradition.

Healing at a distance always involves Gentiles in Matthew. That suggests an interesting connection between this episode and the Roman centurion. Are there other connections? I think that there are. The Gentile woman's kneeling before Jesus was taken, perhaps, as symbolic not only of the Christian mission to the Gentiles but also of the attitude of some Gentiles in prophecy:

Isaiah 49:22-25: Thus says the Lord God: I will soon lift up my hand to the nations, and raise my signal to the peoples; and they shall bring your sons in their bosom, and your daughters shall be carried on their shoulders. Kings shall be your foster fathers, and their queens your nursing mothers. With their faces to the ground they shall bow down to you, and lick the dust of your feet. Then you will know that I am the Lord; those who wait for me shall not be put to shame. Can the prey be taken from the mighty, or the captives of a tyrant be rescued? But thus says the Lord: Even the captives of the mighty shall be taken, and the prey of the tyrant be rescued; for I will contend with those who contend with you, and I will save your children.

Isaiah 60:14: The descendants of those who oppressed you shall come bending low to you, and all who despised you shall bow down at your feet; they shall call you the City of the Lord, the Zion of the Holy One of Israel.

What is honored is confession and humbling. Furthermore, I would argue that Matthew's presentation of the "magi" kneeling before the child in Matthew's birth narrative also alludes strongly to these motifs as well—the East would have represented the lands of all the traditional conquerors of Israel—Babylon, Assyria, and Persia. In the form of the magi, they kneel (Matt. 2:11; Mark 15:19 presents this kneeling of Gentiles in typically ironic form).

If it is true that Mark originally intends to introduce the woman as a person of some means,[8] then we may well be dealing with a woman of greater social standing than Jesus, especially Jesus traveling outside his home territory. Her kneeling renounces her advantage over Jesus, as the centurion renounced his authority over Jesus and other Jews. She is included, I would argue, because Mark (and Matthew) see the Syro-Phoenician woman in the same light as the Roman centurion—a Gentile who renounces power and privilege to follow Jesus. Because of this, both are accepted. Modern concerns about what looks like a rejection of a female ought to be alive to the possible status difference between this woman and Jesus—a status difference that makes Jesus the "lesser," rather than the woman, both by social class and cultural relations.

What I believe we need to do is restore our surprise or shock at the right part of the story. A first-century Jewish reader would not be shocked at Jesus' initial attitude of rejection—they probably would have sympathized. What would have been shocking is the changed message of the passage as a whole—inclusion for repentant Gentiles, healing for repentant Gentiles, and an affirmation of a Gentile's faith—indeed a Gentile *woman's* faith.

SUMMARY: THE MESSAGE OF JESUS IN MATTHEW: RUN THE BORDERS!

The writers of Luke and Matthew both clearly understood the message of Jesus to radically offer hope and light even to the Gentiles. In the end, Matthew presents the Coyote Jesus giving us our directions: "Now run across all borders ..." (i.e., "Go therefore, and make disciples from among all nations" [Matt. 28:19]). This radical violation of national boundaries in mission rather than conquest, and thus Jesus' own radical redefinition of the composition of the kingdom of God, is certainly one of the most powerful aspects of the teachings of Jesus. His nonviolence follows from his openness to others and his hope that enemies can be transformed.

Chapter Seven

Paul and Crossing Borders: The Christian Mandate to the Nations

Every thoughtful person knows that the world needs change. People need to learn new ways to live and especially need to learn to live at peace in open societies that tolerate differences. Of course, many peoples from different religious traditions have different answers to how we can make progress toward these kinds of goals. At their best, Christians also believe that the message of Jesus is a way to bring positive human change—and at their best, this is communicated with modesty and respect. I know that it is not a popular viewpoint among many modern advocates of peace and justice, but I do actually believe in Christian mission: sharing the teachings of Jesus with others. People share teachings they respect all the time; Christians should share their treasures too. I don't believe that mission is inherently wrong, inherently arrogant, or inherently destructive of relationships. It can be, and has been, each of these things and more—but it need not be.

All Christians know that Christianity in general has earned a negative reputation because of some missionary practices of recent centuries. There are, of course, many examples of dedicated missionaries who respected the people and cultures that they lived and worked with and genuinely sought the best for them. Needless to say, I do not agree with destructive or arrogant methods of missionary activity. I most certainly agree with the basic idea of mission, however, and I acknowledge that other religious traditions have just as much right to engage in mission as well.

I also believe dialogue and peacemaking is critically important as Christian action as well as mission. There will be many occasions where sharing our Christian faith may not be appropriate, or occasions where we share our thoughts and receive a friendly (or not-so-friendly) "no thanks." We are not finished being Christians in relation to those who decline our offer to become Christians. We still live and work with all persons, building a peaceful and just society. This is my main criticism of some missionary organizations—they have a tendency to dismiss those who do not respond to mission or want to "move on," as if these people are no longer of interest because they may decline to become Christian. I would say we still have responsibilities to *be* Christians in a just, peaceful, and positive relationship with those who are not Christian. Some Christians, however, do not realize that there is a New Testament theological basis for coexistence with non-Christians, just as there is a New Testament theological basis for mission. Both can be rooted in the thought of Paul.

I think it is very important that two central arguments of Paul be read in light of each other—namely mission and dialogue. This is because when we we read these two issues together, the combination has widespread implications for crossing borders. New Testament readers are familiar with thinking about mission in relation to Paul's thought, but I believe dialogue is also a strong implication of his thought as well. To clarify this, it makes sense to begin with Romans. Paul's letter to the Christians in Rome appears to be one of the only letters in the New Testament written to a church that he did not start and hence was not part of an ongoing conversation. One of the difficulties we have with some of Paul's other letters is that when reading them, we seem to be trying to listen in on half of a telephone conversation. It would have helped to know what the other "party" was saying. With Romans, on the other hand, Paul is initiating the discussion and so he explains himself more fully. This is one reason why Romans has been one of the most influential books in the New

Testament, outside of the Gospels. It is a book that features more or less whole arguments, not partial responses to questions we are not certain of, or parts of conversations between Paul and various church groups.

So why was Romans even written? The first seriously divisive issue that faced early Christianity, and an issue that forced a council for the young Christian movement (described in Acts 15), was the perplexing issue of the relationship of Gentiles and Jews in the movement. The issue was urgent—do "Gentiles" (Greeks) first need to convert to Judaism according to the ritual requirements for this conversion, such as circumcision of males, in order to then be fully Christian? There appear to have been a significant number of Christians in the first century who believed that this was absolutely essential. And, frankly, we can see their point. After all, imagine what some of the more traditional Jewish Christians must have been thinking: What do Greeks know about our God? What could they possibly know of our tradition? Do they know anything about the covenant with Abraham? Do they know anything about Moses and the law? Do they know anything about David or other Messianic expectations of our tradition? Have they read the apocalyptic visions of Daniel? Surely, anyone who seeks to understand Jesus must be a part of Jesus' own faith tradition—or at least know enough to be a convert. How else would they even be able to appreciate who and what Jesus is? These are formidable arguments and serious questions—and they make some sense. Paul obviously had a tough debate on his hands.

The debate may sound like a very old debate that was only important in the first two centuries of Christianity, but it really is not an issue locked in history—it is very much alive in different forms today. The arguments suggesting that Gentiles must become Jews to be real Christians resemble any religious arguments that depend on maintaining rigid borders between "them" and "us." If one of "them" wants to become one of "us" then they will have to stop being one of "them." How many centuries of tragic missionary practice were rooted in the idea that becoming

Christian means becoming like an American or a European: you must sing **our** songs, and wear **our** clothes, and build **our** kind of churches. How many centuries of divisive Christian teachings have insisted on the notion that Christians must worship like "us" and you "others" are not real Christians. It sounds so much like modern political or national resentments toward "others" and their refusal to believe that those "others" have anything good about them. That is when we hear people say things like: "Have you tried to talk to them? You can't reason with them."

Paul, on the other hand, was trying to articulate a theology of crossing borders. From everything we can figure out, Paul was attempting to work out some of the radical implications of what Jesus himself lived and taught. For our purposes, suffice it to say that, in the Epistle to the Romans, Paul is going to try to explain a theology for coyotes—a theological and philosophical defense of the idea of talking to Gentiles and expecting a reasonable response. Paul is about to tell us why Gentiles can be reasoned with. And we understand why this is so important—because Paul wants to establish that Gentiles can be taught, and they can be taught precisely because *they are rather better informed about God and God's ways than we have previously given them credit for.*

At the beginning of Paul's letter to the Christians in Rome, he wants to argue the notion that all people are answerable to God—Jew and Greek. So far, so good. The general circumstance of humanity is that humans have rejected God and are in desperate need to return to a life in relationship with God. But the way his argument proceeds is quite fascinating, and potentially explosive. Let us review the central argument in chapter 2.

> **Romans 2:9-16:** There will be anguish and distress for everyone who does evil, the Jew first and also the Greek, but glory and honor and peace for everyone who does good, the Jew first and also the Greek. For God shows no partiality. All who have sinned apart from the law will also perish apart from the law, and all who have sinned under the law will be judged by the law. For it is not the hearers of the law who are righteous in God's sight, but the doers of the law who will be justified. When Gentiles, who do not possess the law,

do instinctively what the law requires, these, though not having the law, are a law to themselves. They show that what the law requires is written on their hearts, to which their own conscience also bears witness; and their conflicting thoughts will accuse or perhaps excuse them on the day when, according to my gospel, God, through Jesus Christ, will judge the secret thoughts of all.

The real twist in Paul's argument begins at verse 14. He started with negative arguments—most people, whether Jew or Greek, have rejected God. But then he turns to a more positive thought. Imagine a sincere first-century Jewish-Christian in Rome trying to listen intently to Paul's letter being read out in meeting. Paul writes, in so many words: "There were Jews who obeyed the law, and there were Gentiles who obeyed." Fine. On reflection, however, our ancient Christian listener stops and thinks about Paul's word about Gentiles: "Well, wait a moment, what *could* they have obeyed?" So, what could these Gentiles have "obeyed" that was good? Since they did not have the law, didn't God ignore them? Paul says no, God did not ignore them.

Let us be clear about the importance of this debate. Modern Christians often ask serious questions like: "Can people be saved if they are not Christian?" Most of the time, this is the equivalent of asking, "Can a person be good without being one of us?" It is clear that Paul believed that this is quite possible. Jews, according to Paul, have known throughout history what they should do because God taught them through Abraham, Moses, and especially the law and the prophets. Does that mean that Gentiles—that is "the nations"—know nothing? Does that also mean that Gentiles, for example, have never "sinned" because the Hebrew God never told them what was right and what was wrong?

This is precisely the argument that Paul takes on by insisting that Gentiles most certainly *did* know something of the ways of God—Paul says that this knowledge was "written on their hearts." How did it get there? Because God created us all, and God's ways are obvious to anyone who pays attention to how God has made the world:

Romans 1:19-20: For what can be known about God is plain to them, because God has shown it to them. Ever since the creation of the world his eternal power and divine nature, invisible though they are, have been understood and seen through the things he has made. So they are without excuse.

So, do people who have never heard about God in the Mosaic tradition inevitably live a life of sin? Paul says "mostly yes," but concedes that it is possible that non-Jews can act on what they know—they can "live the Jewish law" without even knowing that this is what they are effectively doing. They do this by responding to what they **do** know about God from the way God has made the universe and human society. Paul calls it the "law written on their hearts." It is an interesting argument, and some Christian theologians have drawn from this kind of thinking the notion of a "Natural Law"—a kind of moral code built into the universe. One famous Catholic theologian, Karl Rahner, even spoke of "anonymous Christians"—those whose behavior and life is acceptable to God even if they themselves are not consciously Christian. Paul's radical thinking seems to lead to precisely this kind of observation.

If Paul had believed that Gentiles could **never** understand anything about God, morality, and ultimate issues of faith and practice, then Paul would have never preached his sermon in Athens. This striking sermon appeals not to any basic Jewish concepts but almost entirely to Gentile and Greek concepts and is, therefore, an example of a kind of Christian "creation theology" that applies to any human being:

Acts 17:22-27: Then Paul stood in front of the Areopagus and said, "Athenians, I see how extremely religious you are in every way. For as I went through the city and looked carefully at the objects of your worship, I found among them an altar with the inscription, 'To an unknown god.' What therefore you worship as unknown, this I proclaim to you. The God who made the world and everything in it, he who is Lord of heaven and earth, does not live in shrines made by human hands, nor is he served by human hands, as though he needed anything, since he himself gives to all mortals life and breath and all things. From one ancestor he made all nations to inhabit the whole earth, and he allotted the times of their existence and the boundaries of the places where they would live, so that they would search for God and perhaps grope for him and find him—though indeed he is not far from each one of us."

Did you catch it again? Paul talks about humans of all nations who "grope" for God. The term translated by "grope," incidentally, is used simply to indicate "touch" in other New Testament contexts. (In Luke 24:39, the resurrected Christ asks disciples to "touch" him; 1 John 1:1 talks about a truth "we have touched.") Paul's argument actually allows, in some ways logically demands, that some of these people among the nations can actually "find God." If Paul did not believe Gentiles could become Christians in their own way, Paul would have preached his sermon something like, "Men of Athens, let me explain about Moses," but this is decidedly not what Paul does. Furthermore, Paul even quotes approvingly from Gentile writers and thus builds his case by affirming Gentile insights into the human condition.

> **Acts 17:28:** For "In him we live and move and have our being"; as even some of your own poets have said, "For we too are his offspring."

What can we conclude from this? First, Paul clearly thought it was possible for Gentiles to be righteous before God in the past. Most did not respond to God as they should have, but it was possible that some did. This is hardly revolutionary—we have already seen that there are elements of the Hebrew tradition that tried to argue precisely this kind of thinking. Paul stood in a line of fellow Hebrew coyotes.

Second, however, we can say that in the modern world, Paul's "border violating theology" has some interesting implications. If it was possible to be righteous apart from the law—then is it still possible to be saved without the gospel? What about all the people who have never heard the gospel—both in history and at the present? Are they all lost? Isn't that why Christians should engage in missionary work to the nations?

ISSUES IN COYOTE THEOLOGY: MISSION VERSUS DIALOGUE

What does missionary work—that is, seeking to spread the message of Jesus—have to do with the work of coexistence with others who do not wish to become Christians—what might be called the work of dialogue and tolerance? Now this is an **old** argument between Christian groups in church history, and we cannot go into it deeply here, but we have to wade into these troubled waters just a bit because we Christian coyotes need some clarity on this because of the horrendous damage that Christians have inflicted on the world in the past.

Some Christians believe in missionary work precisely because everyone who has not knowingly responded to the message of Jesus Christ is "lost." Usually this is argued in terms of salvation or eternal status, that is, whether one is going to be with God for eternity. It is clear that those Christians who believe this limited notion of salvation want to maintain a **very** strong border between "them" (all those people who refuse to become Christians for many different reasons) and "us" (all the people who have become Christians in the way considered acceptable by a powerful, usually Western, majority). But just a moment ... what did Paul say in Romans 2:15? Is it possible that the behavior of some of the Gentiles over the previous centuries, even though they were apart from the Jewish law, will actually excuse them when God judges the hearts of all?

That is precisely what Paul believed; namely, people can respond to what they know of God, and this response can be sufficient in the eyes of God. It only stands to reason, of course. Paul's rather cynical, if realistic, view is that most people—Jew and "Greek" (shorthand for all Gentiles)—do **not** respond to God even though they could have. Logically, then, Paul must also acknowledge that it was possible that some people **did** obey "what they knew" of God, and they will be able to be "excused." This is precisely what he does acknowledge. Our message of mission should be this: we are willing to share our belief in Jesus with anyone who may wish to hear, but our message of dialogue and coexistence between all people should be offered to everyone always, Christian or not. We may face rejection of both messages, of course, but our offer of sharing faith must never be imposed or forced, or be unjust or a matter of clever trickery. Here is the interesting point—by mixing these two values: mission and coexistence, it places boundaries on our theology of mission. What I mean is this: mission work must never violate the work of peace and coexistence with all. Mission work that leaves anyone offended, violated, or deceived is not merely a "bad method," it is a flat betrayal of the gospel of Jesus.

I disagree with those who suggest that any kind of mission, any offering of faith, is already a violation of others. I did not consider it offensive at all when a Muslim friend sincerely asked me whether I might consider converting to Islam. I was, in fact, honored to be asked, even as I reassured my friend that I am committed to my Christian faith. We remained friends.

Paul's "coyote theology" has even more serious implications, however, and we can go further. We live in a modern world where virtually everyone has heard the Christian message in one form or another. Sadly, for many millions of human beings since the beginning of the Christian movement, their experience of the Christian message has been tainted with economic greed, colonialist exploitation, military and police violence, or open corruption and greed as indicated by nationalist corruption of church life, the modern building of vast media empires and huge church complexes. It is frankly by the grace of God, for example, that any Native American would embrace Christianity after what was done to most of them by people professing Christianity. It is frankly by the grace of God that Christianity is so centrally important to African Americans when their experience of arriving in the land of America was mostly an experience of "Christian" slave traders and owners. It is frankly by the grace of God that the Maori of New Zealand or Aboriginal Australians embraced Christianity despite the land grabbing and violence from European settlers. We could go on. In sum, we have to confess that for many modern people the kind of patient thought that is willing to overlook the grave sins and behavior of the Christians in order to see the core message of Jesus himself is expecting more than most Western Christians would themselves be willing to tolerate. Consider, for example, the self-righteous Christian criticism of some examples of bad Islamic behavior in the modern world. What conveniently short memories Christians can have.

I believe that modern Christians must acknowledge that for many modern people to try to see the teachings and person of Jesus directly—despite the behavior of many self-professed Christians—often presents them with a credibility gap that is impossible to cross. This is a credibility gap between what Christians say they believe and how they actually live—and it can be so great that the Christian message can lose virtually any appeal it may have had. This is deeply tragic. It is sad that to this day we have Christians who continue with offensive, childish, or simplistic missionary strategies, blithely excusing the nonsense by saying, "We will do whatever works," ignoring the horrendous damage they are doing not only to human beings, but also to the Christian message itself.

What does it mean when, for example, a Native American man or woman rejects Christianity when their only experience of it has been accompanied by oppression and exploitation? Can we blame anyone for saying, "If that is the religion you people profess, there must be something deeply wrong with it." I believe that Paul's teaching is that such persons can still respond to God in their own way—and many clearly have. Quite frankly, this is something that I am deeply relieved about—God's relationships with humanity are not always dependent upon our failed attempts to live the gospel. I believe with Paul that when we all face God, there will be forms of faith outside Christianity that are authentic responses to "the God they know," and those forms of faith will, in the words of Paul, "excuse them." It is the height of arrogance to proclaim to all people who have rejected Christianity—especially those who have rejected it because of the horrendous behavior of the

Christian people—that they are lost. Paul's reasoning in Romans and Acts says that many non-Christians are not lost. If a Buddhist, Hindu, or Muslim's understanding of God or spirituality is deeply offended by the behavior of violent Christians, then no wonder they reject the invitation to convert. When American missionaries accept military assistance (travel in military escorts or vehicles) and thus present to non-Western peoples a picture of "Jesus and the American guns"—are we surprised when Christianity is rejected? Are those who reject such a pathetic image of Jesus **lost**? It is not for me to say, of course, what anyone's individual relationship to God may be. In the end, of course, one's relationship to God and the cosmos is not my business. What I do know, however, is that it is quite possible that a person can reject a horribly distorted Christianity and yet still respond, in the words of Paul, to "the law written on their hearts," and this response may well take the form of other faith traditions.

Therefore, in the modern age, we have a biblical basis for mission *and* dialogue. Dialogue is accepting the possibility that our presentation is wrong or has failed or that others simply prefer the superiority of their own tradition and their own way. We then should practice our openness to learn from other viewpoints. They can still respond to God as they understand God, and dialogue respects this. Dialogue also presumes a commitment to coexistence.

Even further, however, I believe Paul's theology allows even more important developments for modern Christians. A non-Christian's faith may be deeper than our own. What I mean is this—a Jew or Muslim or Buddhist's spiritual faith may have profound truths to teach a facile, simplistic Christian faith. If I believe that Christianity is the clearest expression of God in human experience, that does not mean that my *own* version of Christianity is the best or clearest. Far from it. I am deeply grateful for the profound spiritual insights I have gained from those whose non-Christian faith is more mature than my Christian faith. Coexistence is not merely "tolerance," it invites the possibility of sharing, interaction, and profound fellowship as we listen to each other. Paul, when he first read Greek philosophers, was so struck by some of their insights that he memorized their thoughts. This is why they came to mind as he shared his own faith tradition in Athens.

Does the call to dialogue and respectful coexistence mean the end of all motivation for missionary work? Not at all. Paul's main point still stands—most people reject God and need to be called upon and offered a path to God. I believe Christianity must never be forced on anyone, but it should be available as a choice to anyone. Christians should respect hearing: "No, thank you" as the answer to their offer of sharing their faith. Finally, however, I would offer this word: the most powerful "mission" for the twenty-first century would be to actually live the peaceful gospel of Jesus. Perhaps we should stop talking, hoping people will be convinced by arguments, and realize that many people in spiritual crisis may be waiting to see a gospel actually lived. Maybe they are waiting for coyotes.

A "Pauline"-type coyote theology, therefore, includes an ability to affirm the "other"—either as partner or convert. This obviously has implications for issues of Christians and violence. Some of these implications are drawn by Paul himself in the same letter to the Romans:

> **Romans 12:14-21:** Bless those who persecute you; bless and do not curse them. Rejoice with those who rejoice, weep with those who weep. Live in harmony with one another; do not be haughty, but associate with the lowly; do not claim to be wiser than you are. Do not repay anyone evil for evil, but take thought for what is noble in the sight of all. If it is possible, so far as it depends on you, live peaceably with all. Beloved, never avenge yourselves, but leave room for the wrath of God; for it is written, "Vengeance is mine, I will repay, says the Lord." No, "if your enemies are hungry, feed them; if they are thirsty, give them something to drink; for by doing this you will heap burning coals on their heads." Do not be overcome by evil, but overcome evil with good.

It is now widely acknowledged that Paul is likely actually quoting Jesus in many of these sayings, and Jesus is the source of the "spirit" of this entire important passage. There have also been some interesting questions about Paul's use of the Proverb regarding heaping "coals on their heads." Some believe that Paul is speaking of an eventual judgment on those who are evil. This is possible after all. The New Testament does acknowledge that evil will not be forever tolerated by God. But is this what Paul means by quoting Proverbs 25:21-22? Note a purifying effect, as when a coal purifies the lips of the prophet Isaiah:

> **Isaiah 6:6-7:** Then one of the seraphs flew to me, holding a live coal that had been taken from the altar with a pair of tongs. The seraph touched my mouth with it and said: "Now that this has touched your lips, your guilt has departed and your sin is blotted out."

But this need not distract us from the main point—Paul's theology of violating borders between groups of people in the name of the gospel of Jesus Christ leads quite naturally to a deep understanding of, and commitment to, ending violence and warfare. The effort to "feed" your enemy, incidentally, is quite likely an appeal to justice issues. Jesus himself, in another interesting context of judgment, talked about feeding and giving drink to people that were obviously not considered worthwhile by some:

> **Matthew 25:34-40:** Then the king will say to those at his right hand, "Come, you that are blessed by my Father, inherit the kingdom prepared for you from the foundation of the world; for I was hungry and you gave me food, I was thirsty and you gave me something to drink, I was a stranger and you welcomed me, I was naked and you gave me clothing, I was sick and you took care of me, I was in prison and you visited me." Then the righteous will answer him, "Lord, when was it that we saw you hungry and gave you food, or thirsty and gave you something to drink? And when was it that we saw you a stranger and welcomed you, or naked and gave you clothing? And when was it that we saw you sick or in prison and visited you?" And the king will answer them, "Truly I tell you, just as you did it to one of the least of these who are members of my family, you did it to me."

The passage from Matthew does include judgment for those who refused to engage with "the least of these." Once again, we are called upon to take seriously the significance of the language of judgment as the language of significant issues. It is quite interesting to me how the harsh language of judgment in the New Testament can often be cited as offensive and troubling by the same folks who take quite seriously the importance of working for social justice. To struggle for social justice is to recognize that there are enemies of justice and enemies of honesty and enemies of sharing. To struggle for justice, even nonviolently, is to engage in a conflict. However, many Christians deeply committed to peace and justice have serious difficulties with the language of conflict and judgment in the New Testament—even in the service of peace and justice. It is to this issue that we must turn because the New Testament itself ends in a flurry of angry language.

Chapter Eight

The Harps of Pacifism or the Hammers of Nonviolence?

The imagery I am using for the title of this chapter—harps and hammers—is taken from a speech by Kurt Hiller in 1920. Hiller, born in 1885, was a Jewish intellectual during the fascinating German progressive political debates between the world wars about the future of German society. In this notable speech against war, Hiller (certainly himself a border crosser of some serious literary accomplishment) challenges the stereotypes about nonviolence by starting his speech:

> Honored comrades in the struggle ... or would some among you suppose that this is an improper form of address for pacifists, thinking that pacifism and struggle are mutually exclusive? I disagree in the strongest terms. Pacifism is not a peaceful skill.[1]

In this striking speech that I have frequently thought about over the years, Hiller cites the example of Jesus in the Temple, ejecting the animals and overturning tables. Hiller cites this episode approvingly, asserting that nonviolence is active, engaged, and serious about change in the world:

> It seems to me that too few pacifists hold a whip!... We have the duty before the Spirit, not to leave undone that which, if done, and done suitably, will accelerate the end of the era of mass murder and the age of warfare from this planet. *We do not have a pacifist's harp to pluck, but rather a pacifist hammer to swing!*[2]

Hiller's challenge is fascinating—he uses quite forceful language to speak of the responsibility of antiwar activism. But it is his imagery that I find especially fascinating, and memorable. Can imagery be dangerous? And how does this relate to violent language in the Bible?

No matter how convincing any argument may be about the nonviolence of the teaching and life of Jesus, the remaining problem is always the final book of the Bible: the violent, troubling Apocalypse of John, or Revelation. Does this violent language somehow unravel all arguments for the New Testament teachings on peace and nonviolence? I believe that Revelation, too, has its place in the practice of Christian nonviolence. To understand why this is the case, however, will require that we once again return to the Old Testament to understand the language of violence, and violent language.

Biblical scholars have known for centuries that Revelation is not an unusual book. It seems to be unusual only because it is the only example of this kind of Jewish literature that appears in the New Testament (although Jesus, at times, uses language that sounds a bit like Revelation, such as the speech in Matthew 24, but also in shorter sayings, such as Matt. 16:27-28). In the form of literature known as *apocalyptic,* violent imagery and language is not unusual, especially imagery and language about judgment and punishments of the wicked. But is violent language and imagery the same thing as violent actions? Clearly one can accompany the other ... but not always.

One of the most important difficulties of speaking of nonviolence in the Bible is the recognition that nonviolence at least **seems** to be incompatible with the imagery of violence and war that we find even in the New Testament. I want to argue, however, that this is a false perception—angry rhetoric is not incompatible with nonviolence. In fact, it is precisely those who *oppose* Christian pacifism and nonviolence who most often criticize Christian advocates of nonviolence for their "angry" tone. Is anger only for the warriors? We pacifists are apparently banned from sounding serious about our work, much less getting angry.

We apparently must abandon the language of gritty realism when speaking of peacemaking. To accept this stereotype, of course, is to accept the attempts to make peacemaking irrelevant. The writers of the New Testament, however, have other ideas.

The truth is different, both historically and biblically. In fact, there is a long and rich tradition of violent imagery that can accompany pacifist activism. The early Quakers spoke of their own engagement in nonviolent preaching and social change by coining the term, "The Lamb's War" (borrowed from imagery in Revelation). The Salvation Army is a Christian church that addresses its leaders as officers who have "ranks" in their spiritual militia. Among the founding generation of the Salvationists was Arthur Sydney Booth-Clibborn, who wrote a strong antiwar tract entitled, "Blood against Blood" (1901). His was not a perfumed, wistful dreaming—but a hard-hitting condemnation of the greed that fuels warfare. Other examples of strong rhetoric in peacemaking illustrate the point. For example, the philosopher William James delivered his famous speech, "The Moral Equivalent of War" at Stanford University in 1906, arguing that the same discipline and training that is wasted on warfare ought to be "marshaled" for the "war" against human backwardness. He was a strongly committed antiwar philosopher, but used the **language** of war to assert the significance of discipline, organization of effort, and preparedness similar to warfare itself. Some attribute the founding of service "corps" in American history (e.g., Peace Corps; Job Corps; AmeriCorps) to James's influence. The point was, he used military imagery to speak of nonviolent values—and spoke as an avowed pacifist. Finally, many modern Islamic advocates of nonviolence (of which there are many, despite Western prejudices that Islam is always violent) speak frequently of the Muslim concept of the inward jihad—the spiritual war against sin in one's own soul—as the superior war over physical, outward jihad. All of these traditions draw on militant images for nonviolent ends. I believe that it is in this context that we must understand not only the violent language of the last book of the Bible but also Paul's use of warfare imagery such as the following passage:

Ephesians 6:13-17: Therefore take up the whole armor of God, so that you may be able to withstand on that evil day, and having done everything, to stand firm. Stand therefore, and fasten the belt of truth around your waist, and put on the breastplate of righteousness. As shoes for your feet put on whatever will make you ready to proclaim the gospel of peace. With all of these, take the shield of faith, with which you will be able to quench all the flaming arrows of the evil one. Take the helmet of salvation, and the sword of the Spirit, which is the word of God.

But Paul makes very clear that his military rhetoric must not be misunderstood—he is not advocating actual, physical warfare:

Ephesians 6:12: For our struggle is not against enemies of blood and flesh, but against the rulers, against the authorities, against the cosmic powers of this present darkness, against the spiritual forces of evil in the heavenly places.

Admittedly, we are in murky waters here. There are many modern Christian leaders who believe that the very language of violence and warfare is dangerous. Feminist scholars, particularly, often assert that the language of domination and control has contributed to male attitudes that encourage the oppression and physical abuse of women. It is dangerous to somehow equate physical strength with the moral right to act against the wishes of those physically less capable of defending themselves. Note how often even consensual sex is informally referred to by many men as "conquering" a woman. Language can be dangerous, and I quite agree that language can also be abusive and may contribute to violent acts. But is this inevitable?

Further, many feminist biblical scholars have asked whether the language of abuse against women (Hosea 2, for example) may actually encourage modern readers to believe that such attitudes of domination and control are not only permitted but also openly encouraged.[3] Many readers of ancient texts point out that metaphors can be dangerous—and verbal abuse (bad in itself) can also become physical abuse. So far, I quite agree. There is, however, more to be said, especially when reading ancient documents and dealing across cultures. Verbal violence turned against another human being can be a weapon wielded with devastating results, but can violent imagery and rhetoric be directed against concepts and ideas? Can the realism of nonviolent responses to evil also employ the language of determined commitment that can even marshal (!) the *language* of warfare? Paul seemed to accept the notion that spiritual warfare can use the language of military encounter and training. Does this rhetorical strategy invariably create the conditions of violence? Is there a possibility that violent imagery can accompany nonviolent intentions—and indeed further such nonviolent intentions?

I agree that we must face the dangers of angry and violent rhetoric but affirm, at the same time, that violent imagery does not always and inevitably mean that the person speaking in such language approves of **actual** violence. In fact, the use of violent rhetoric can actually draw on the surrounding cultural and historical realities in a manner that effectively turns these images against destructive behaviors. It is in this spirit that I believe we must examine some of the "war rhetoric" of the Bible, both Old and New Testaments.

Finally, there is one further observation. As someone who has lived for short periods in my life in circumstances where political and social injustice, violence, and oppression were, and are, close at hand, I am familiar with the fact that angry rhetoric has a function not often appreciated in Western societies where polite speech is treasured as the sign of both a cultured and an educated background. There is an elite sense of "being nice" that is violated by the anger of social unrest. Too often the Western press exploits the use of angry rhetoric of movements for social change as a means to discredit the movement and its goals. I still remember, as a fairly traditional white Euro-American boy growing up in mainly white southeast Portland, what a shock it was to be assigned a provocative book in high school: *The Autobiography of Malcolm X.* The fury of some of Malcolm X's words startled me, but I came to understand that sometimes angry words express deep-seated emotions over real issues. Still, many of my young friends were upset with the rhetoric. Witness the advent of the language of "Black Power" in the United States—and the tradition of anger that continues in some forms of rap music in modern African American expression.

EPHESIANS 6 AS "POWER LANGUAGE"?

The rise of the phrase "Black Power" is associated with one of the most radical of the early 1960s Civil Rights groups, known as the Student Nonviolent Coordinating Committee (usually referred to simply as "Snick," pronouncing the acronym SNCC). The irony that the phrase arose within an organization bearing the words "nonviolent" is, of course, part of the fascinating history of SNCC.[4]

The name usually associated with the move toward the use of the phrase "Black Power" is the fiery activist Stokely Carmichael, who died in Africa as the renamed Kwame Ture in November 1998. Claybourne Carson, the noted editor of the Dr. King papers, writes of the initial rhetorical changes toward the use of the phrase "Black Power" by suggesting that it was motivated by frustration:

> Disillusioned by their previous attempts to achieve change through nonviolent tactics and interracial alliances, Carmichael and other outspoken militants in SNCC were no longer restrained by concern for the sensibilities of white people. By forthrightly expressing previously suppressed anger, Carmichael and others experienced a sense of "release" similar to that felt by black activists during the early days of the lunch counter sit-in movement.... *SNCC workers' satisfaction with the black power slogan was based largely on the extent to which it aroused blacks and disturbed whites....* [my emphasis][5]

Christopher Strain further comments:

> When Carmichael and Ricks introduced ... the phrase "Black Power," they alarmed white folks ... [but] ... for most black folks, the appeal of Black Power lay in its excitement and energy, not its

threat.... But as the notion of Black Power expanded and took on a life of its own, some black activists used its ominous overtones as a loosely veiled threat to whites.... Conceptions of Black Power were hazy at best, and the phrase clearly meant different things to different people.[6]

Carson is careful to point out that Carmichael's statements of policy never advocated violence, much less advocated unrestrained, frustrated rage, but at the same time, he was keenly aware of the power of the rhetorical move toward the use of the phrase "Black Power." Strain, along these lines, observes that:

Black Power was an Afro-American expression of political and social empowerment, rather than an ideology of racial supremacy. It is worth nothing that, for most activists being pro-black did not mean being anti-white.[7]

Carmichael, writes Strain, was quoted as saying, "When you build your own house, it doesn't mean you tear down the house across the street."[8] Further, Strain uses the terms, "self-determination," "self-sufficiency," and "self-protection" as terms that speak to the heart of the meaning of Black Power in the context of the early 1960s Civil Rights movement.[9] Carson notes the observations of the black psychiatrist Alvin Poussaint, who observed that those who used the phrase *Black Power* "appeared to be seeking a sense of psychological emancipation from racism through self assertion and release of aggressive angry feelings."[10]

What is undeniable, however, is the power of the rhetoric itself. In Carson's concluding observations about the legacy of SNCC in the Civil Rights movement, he notes that Carmichael's use of what other Civil Rights historians have referred to as "the rhetoric of rage" had a powerful impact: "Stokely Carmichael had been one of SNCC's most effective organizers, but his fiery speeches rather than his activities in Mississippi and Alabama made him a nationally known leader."[11]

The amount of actual violence inspired by the language of "Black Power" is one of the ongoing debates about the Civil Rights movement. Strain even makes the fascinating observation that talk **about** guns was "more serviceable as rhetorical appendages than as tools of revolution, or even as devices of self-protection."[12]

The reactions were obvious. Carson (and others) suggest that police and especially FBI involvement in civil rights issues took on a new level of earnestness following the rise of the angry rhetoric—and not necessarily because of the rise of actual incidents of violence (and certainly not as a result of the already decades-old levels of violence directed against African-Americans).

The point that I wish to draw attention to with this very briefly drawn "case study" is the actual power of the rhetoric of violence and its various "functions" within a social context. Words express anger, and as such can be considered a release of emotion, but they also express a verbal form of force, and thus rhetoric itself has a certain kind of power—as Strain pointedly observes, words *about* guns were arguably more powerful than the guns themselves. This is, in my view, a radically important way to read Paul's use of military imagery, and Revelation's angry use of apocalyptic images.

There are other examples, of course. Angry rhetoric was (and is) also a common mode of expression in the rise of the American Indian Movement—and yet one must contrast the angry **imagery** of a Native founder of AIM like Dennis Banks with the gentle spirit expressed in his autobiography.[13] In his writing, he described his strong advocacy against **actual** violence during the frightening events at Wounded Knee that could have ended far more violently than they did. Here, one must learn to acknowledge that anger is an important expression of real problems, real issues, and matters of highly emotional importance. The examples could be multiplied indefinitely. Is there a problem with the use of angry rhetoric? Theorists of social movements will now clearly state that the selection of language and style are essential matters of careful thought and planning—but it is hard to avoid the conclusion that angry images can have their intended impact. I wish to be clear in my use of these examples. I am not arguing that all uses of "Black Power" or "Red Power" were examples of pacifist rhetoric. When connected to justice issues, we often evaluate "power" language differently. We must always guard against the temptation, visible in some polemics from Cold War rhetoric to radical feminist rhetoric, that somehow suggests that "my angry rhetoric is just," while "your angry rhetoric" is dangerous. What I am arguing, however, is that forceful and even violent imagery may not always and in all times be contrary to a biblical and thus nonviolent commitment.

Furthermore, even though anger has not been something that has been seriously studied in human experience until rather recently, some historians have observed that there were times when expressions of anger were considered appropriate to certain social positions and political authorities.

Writing about medieval commentators on the anger of kings, historian Stephen White notes:

> Public displays of anger are almost always made by kings or other males whose noble status entitles them to express anger; the displays occur in a limited number of predictable settings. The settings are predictable because displays of anger can usually be read as conventionalized responses to certain kinds of past political acts, as political acts in themselves, and as motives for future political acts of certain kinds.[14]

In the same collection of essays on anger in medieval thought, Paul Freedman makes the interesting observation that, although a king's anger was justified and proper, peasant anger was not: "Comic or murderous, peasant anger was quintessentially irrational."[15] What this means is that in certain cultures (including the past in Western culture) there are times when anger seems an appropriate response. Even today, if we go to an authority figure with a complaint, we feel somehow better if this person acts indignant at the "injustice" that we have suffered and promises to investigate. If anger isn't at least feigned, we feel that the issue is not being taken seriously. There are other locations of social experience, however, where we can expect angry rhetoric—typically in situations where injustice and oppression has taken place. What this means is that anyone working for social change will often be in contact with people who have suffered injustices and unfair practices, and these same people often express their suffering in the language and rhetoric of anger and even violent images. I believe that it may have some therapeutic role, but I leave that to the social psychologists to work out. (The psychologist and revolutionary writer Frantz Fanon wrote of this subject in his classic work, *The Wretched of the Earth*, first published in 1961.) What I think is important, however, is that we take these insights about angry imagery, and come to terms with some of the power of biblical imagery of war and violence. Let us explore why this is important.

BIBLICAL HISTORY AND THE RHETORIC OF VIOLENCE

Let us begin by reminding ourselves that the biblical historians who wrote and edited the books we call Joshua, Judges, 1–2 Samuel, and 1–2 Kings, were writing a single historical work. These six books are often called "The Deuteronomistic History" because of their literary and chronological associations with the book of Deuteronomy. This massive work consists of six of the mainly "historical books" in our Bible (not counting 1–2 Chronicles, which is another historical work from a much later time).

This means that the writer of the six-book history from Joshua to 2 Kings was not merely recording history (apparently it was already recorded in older sources) but was making a point by citing selections from older works and, therefore, attempting to teach lessons by citing **selected** historical events. What are some of these lessons? What motivated the writers of this great work? In order to get a sense of this, we must first ask a very important question: when were these books finally finished in the form that we have them?

These historical books do not indicate when they were written, of course. Perhaps there is a workable solution to the question, however. If you were handed a general "History of the United States" or "History of Australia" and the title pages were missing, how would you discover roughly when this book was finished? The obvious answer is to read the last event described in the history book. Presumably, this last event is roughly the time of the writer, because he or she stops there. The last major event at the end of 2 Kings is a description of the fall of Jerusalem to the Babylonian forces:

> **2 Kings 25:8-12:** In the fifth month, on the seventh day of the month—which was the nineteenth year of King Nebuchadnezzar, king of Babylon—Nebuzaradan, the captain of the bodyguard, a servant of the king of Babylon, came to Jerusalem. He burned the house of the LORD, the king's house, and all the houses of Jerusalem; every great house he burned down. All the army of the Chaldeans who were with the captain of the guard broke down the walls around Jerusalem. Nebuzaradan the captain of the guard carried into exile the rest of the people who were left in the city and the deserters who had defected to the king of Babylon—all the rest of the population. But the captain of the guard left some of the poorest people of the land to be vinedressers and tillers of the soil.

What we have, then, is a narrative of Israelite history that begins with the entry into the land under Joshua and finishes with the destruction of Jerusalem by the Babylonians (roughly the period covered between 1230 BCE and 587 BCE). *But it is a history written after the fall of Jerusalem and in the shadow of the crisis caused by the conquest of Judah and Jerusalem.* It is not merely a dull, uninterested recitation of events. It is a carefully constructed work that seeks to make some significant religious and ethical points in the light of one of the most significant changes of circumstances that the ancient Hebrews ever faced—the destruction of Jerusalem and the Babylonian Exile of many of the leaders of the Judean peoples. One of the main questions being asked was clearly: how could God have allowed this? We have seen quite often that the classic answers given by the historical books of the Bible, probably inspired by the prophet Jeremiah, is: "We are at fault! Especially our kings and rulers." As we know, this certainly did echo the teaching of the Prophet Jeremiah, who taught that the people's sin resulted in God sending the Babylonians to rule for a period. Jeremiah said that the Judeans would have to "wear the iron yoke" of Babylon (Jeremiah 28) because of their sins, but this language is also found in the warnings of Deuteronomy 28. According to Deuteronomy, what will happen if the people do not serve God according to the laws of Moses?

> **Deuteronomy 28:47-52:** Because you did not serve the LORD your God joyfully and with gladness of heart for the abundance of everything, therefore you shall serve your enemies whom the LORD will send against you, in hunger and thirst, in nakedness and lack of everything. He will put an iron yoke on your neck until he has destroyed you. The LORD will bring a nation from far away, from the end of the earth, to swoop down on you like an eagle, a nation whose language you do not understand, a grim-faced nation showing no respect to the old or favor to the young. It shall consume the fruit of your livestock and the fruit of your ground until you are destroyed, leaving you neither grain, wine, and oil, nor the increase of your cattle and the issue of your flock, until it has made you perish. It shall besiege you in all your towns until your high and fortified walls, in which you trusted, come down throughout your land; it shall besiege you in all your towns throughout the land that the LORD your God has given you.

Scholars still debate when this part of Deuteronomy 28 was written, but one thing is clear—the historical books clearly intended to survey Israelite history and through this survey try to show that the exile was the result of sin. In other words, what was warned about in Deuteronomy 28 came to pass, especially in the events described at the end of 2 Kings. How does all this relate to the question of war and peace in the Bible? Let us direct our thinking toward the descriptions of warfare that we find in these historical books.

THE PORTRAYAL OF MIRACLE WAR AND THE RISE OF THE MONARCHY

We find most descriptions of conventional wars in ancient Israel in the historical accounts of 1–2 Samuel and 1–2 Kings after the establishment of the kings. By conventional war, I mean descriptions of conflict that seem to describe ancient hostilities in entirely understandable terms: armies prepare for battle, engage each other, and the stronger force or the superior strategies win out. Often it is siege warfare rather than open-field battles, but the descriptions (while usually quite brief) seem to be unremarkable. For example, in 2 Samuel 10:1-19, there seems to be more interest in the cause of the battle than describing the strategies, weaponry, and conduct of the battle.

And often the description of battle warrants very little comment at all, other than noting that something happened. The very next passage after the battle cited above summarizes another battle in a mere few phrases:

> **2 Samuel 11:1:** In the spring of the year, the time when kings go out to battle, David sent Joab with his officers and all Israel with him; they ravaged the Ammonites, and besieged Rabbah. But David remained at Jerusalem.

Of course, these historical descriptions are rarely objective—they are partisan, and the Biblical descriptions make no pretense about taking sides in the battle descriptions—there are clear "good guys" and clear "bad guys" in most battle scenes. In 2 Samuel 10, David was obviously offended at the treatment of his envoys sent to Ammon. In 2 Samuel 11, however, it seems to simply suggest that anger continued with further battles. This does not seem entirely unusual as a description of warfare in the Bible. It is also interesting to know that the Bible shares many aspects of writing battle reports that were used by other ancient Near Eastern peoples throughout the region. In a fascinating study, K. Lawson Younger compared Biblical "battle reports" with ancient reports from the empires of the Assyrians, Hittites, and Egyptians.[16] He discovered that there were lots of common themes in each of them:

- Our gods assisted in our glorious victory;
- there were huge numbers of enemy killed;
- the enemies were terrified at our wondrous power and armies, etc.

One of Younger's most interesting conclusions is that many biblical battle scenes follow a set pattern inspired by highlighting God's leading rather than human involvement. However, there is an interesting mystery raised by paying attention to the patterns and themes of biblical battle reports. Consider a description of a "battle" like the following, which describes the opening sequence of the Crossing of the Sea episode of the Exodus story. In this text, the Israelites saw the approaching chariots of Pharaoh and were terrified. But consider what Moses suggests:

> **Exodus 14:13-14:** But Moses said to the people, "Do not be afraid, stand firm, and see the deliverance that the LORD will accomplish for you today; for the Egyptians whom you see today you shall never see again. The LORD will fight for you, and you have only to keep still."

Now this is unusual. Among the standard patterns of reporting battles throughout the ancient world, including the Bible, was to claim that our "gods" helped us with the battle. We have many inscriptions from ancient empires bragging that their gods assisted them in victory. It is clear that the Bible also shares this idea that God is a "God of War" and frequently attributes victory to God's assistance:

> **2 Samuel 22:1-4:** David spoke to the LORD the words of this song on the day when the LORD delivered him from the hand of all his enemies, and from the hand of Saul. He said: The LORD is my rock, my fortress, and my deliverer, my God, my rock, in whom I take refuge, my shield and the horn of my salvation, my stronghold and my refuge, my savior; you save me from violence. I call upon the LORD, who is worthy to be praised, and I am saved from my enemies.

In the passage from Exodus, however, the idea seems to be that God will "fight" a war with Pharaoh and his armies entirely alone—without any human assistance from the Israelites. What kind of war description is this? In fact, what kind of *war* is this?

The Mennonite Old Testament scholar Millard Lind is widely noted for most effectively pointing out that the biblical historical books contain highly unusual descriptions of "miraculous" warfare, but that these "miracle wars" (or Yahweh Wars) occur largely before the establishment of the monarchy. In these kinds of war, God fights alone, or with ridiculously minimal assistance.[17]

There are two particularly important examples of these kinds of miracle wars in the pre-kingship period of biblical history, according to the books of Joshua and Judges. The first example is, of course, the battle for Jericho. The Israeli general and archaeologist Yigael Yadin writes with almost hilarious understatement when he describes the biblical story of Jericho, which in his view: "describes another kind of stratagem whose military implications, however, have been obscure."[18] Obscure, indeed. The actual fall of the city is narrated using highly unconventional tactics:

> **Joshua 6:15-16, 20:** On the seventh day they rose early, at dawn, and marched around the city in the same manner seven times. It was only on that day that they marched around the city seven times. And at the seventh time, when the priests had blown the trumpets, Joshua said to the people, "Shout! For the LORD has given you the city...." So the people shouted, and the trumpets were blown. As soon as the people heard the sound of the trumpets, they raised a great shout, and the wall fell down flat; so the people charged straight ahead into the city and captured it.

One is tempted to remark that the military "strategy" in the battle of Jericho is not merely obscure in this passage, it is absent. But just to be sure that we get the point, let us briefly consider the other important example in Judges 7, the "battle" between Gideon and the Midianites. Once again, the preparations for battle are highly irregular. Gideon, as a good military leader, thinks he should gather up thirty-two thousand soldiers. But God takes Gideon by surprise, it would seem, with the following instructions:

> **Judges 7:2-3:** The LORD said to Gideon, "The troops with you are too many for me to give the Midianites into their hand. Israel would only take the credit away from me, saying, 'My own hand

has delivered me.' Now therefore proclaim this in the hearing of the troops, 'Whoever is fearful and trembling, let him return home.'" Thus Gideon sifted them out; twenty-two thousand returned, and ten thousand remained.

Gideon has just lost two-thirds of his army. Yet, the army still has too many in it. The passage continues:

Judges 7:4-6: Then the LORD said to Gideon, "The troops are still too many; take them down to the water and I will sift them out for you there. When I say, 'This one shall go with you,' he shall go with you; and when I say, 'This one shall not go with you,' he shall not go." So he brought the troops down to the water; and the LORD said to Gideon, "All those who lap the water with their tongues, as a dog laps, you shall put to one side; all those who kneel down to drink, putting their hands to their mouths, you shall put to the other side." The number of those that lapped was three hundred; but all the rest of the troops knelt down to drink water.

What is the "military strategy" here? The strategy here, too, is somewhat obscure. Even though the nonmilitary strategy is not immediately obvious to many, there have been readers of the Bible convinced that there is a realistic battle tactic in these kinds of passages.

In their book *Battles of the Bible*, Chaim Herzog, at one time director of military intelligence for Israel, and Mordechai Gichon, an Israeli military historian, attempt to derive an actual strategy:

By a spark of inspiration, Gideon chose his small task force by observing the habits and behaviour of his men while we led them in full daylight to the spring of Harod ... the men chosen were those who, in spite of their thirst, remained cautious of the presence of the enemy nearby and did not abandon their weapons even when drinking, which they managed to do by lying down upon their bellies and lapping up the water, which they gathered in one cupped hand, with their tongues.[19]

Now, this notion that Gideon reduced his army to some kind of elite force of three hundred has a long history and is often cited by those who wish to derive realistic strategy from the biblical accounts. Gichon and Herzog cite their source as the observations of General Sir Archibald P. Wavell, who was for a time commander in chief of British soldiers in the Middle East and based in Egypt during World War II. In Wavell's 1948 book, *The Good Soldier,* he proposed this reading of Gideon's battle as a master strategy of selecting three hundred soldiers to accomplish what thirty-two thousand could not achieve. It is, of course, a seriously flawed reading of the story. The text itself identifies the three hundred remaining soldiers as an army of fools ("like dogs"). If any soldiers were prepared for battle, it was surely the ones who knelt down on one knee, rather than those three hundred who flopped on their stomachs and drank like dogs. Although Gichon and Herzog strain to describe how physically lying flat on your stomach actually allows you to remain cautious and ready for battle, it is clear that such attempts to make these battle reports more realistic are seriously missing the point. Surely the point of comparing them to dogs is that they were not the slightest bit prepared for battle. The observation, rather, is that Gideon was to be sent with the least likely rabble that he could possibly have— precisely because the writer of the Bible wants to emphasize that **God** was the power of victory, and not human strength at all. To derive strategies from these accounts of miracle war is to read against the very theology of the biblical text itself. These are descriptions of miraculous events. One can express serious doubt about the historicity of these miracles, of course, but what one cannot do is deny that this is what the text is talking about and try to transform them into serious strategy.

Equally misleading is the tendency of some of these same books that try to analyze the military strategies of the Bible and often publish fanciful charts and maps (e.g., showing "troop movements"), complete with arrows on relief maps claiming to show the movements of armies, as if the miraculous military campaigns like the fall of Jericho and Gideon's battle with the Midianites can be realistically traced and followed on a chart. The actual details of the story, of course, reduce military strategy to a nonsense. This is precisely the point of the biblical story. God engaged in the conflict by means of miracle, not human plans or strategies. We may try to reduce the textual emphasis on miracle by drawing World War II–type "troop movement" maps in Bible atlases, but this is arguably a forced interpretation masquerading as historical analysis. If we wanted to draw a true "battle map" of the Jericho conflict, for example, it would have to appear so silly that no Bible atlas will ever publish it:[20]

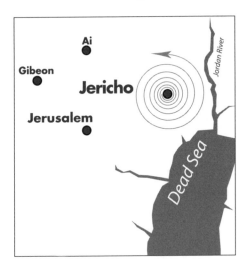

Let us return to our question: why do the writers of the historical books of the Bible portray many of the battles fought before the rise of kingship as miraculous battles won by the power of God, usually minimizing any human involvement at all? The answer is directly related to the timing of the final writing of these books—in the aftermath of the events of the exile. The writers want to suggest that in the times when we "trusted God" (before we chose a king to fight our battles by conventional means) God actually took care of us—God even fought our battles. Since the Israelite peoples were in exile, or under severe occupation back in Palestine, from the time of 587 BCE, the notion of mounting major armies like the time of the kings of Israel was hardly a realistic option. If there was ever a time when they needed God to intervene directly, miraculously, for a weakened people, surely it was the time after 587 BCE.

Descriptions in the Bible: Rhetoric of Anger or Strategy of Fighting?

While there are some humorous aspects of these miracle war descriptions (especially the Gideon story), the subject becomes deadly serious when we come to descriptions of the tactics of some of these wars. We speak here, of course, of the subject of the genocidal practice of "the ban." The description in many of these stories reports the killing of all living things. An example is the description that followed the destruction of the walls of Jericho: "Then they devoted to destruction by the edge of the sword all in the city, both men and women, young and old, oxen, sheep, and donkeys" (Josh. 6:21).

What is particularly perplexing, however, is the fact that these biblical descriptions of the genocidal tactic usually translated as the *ban* (in biblical Hebrew, the *herem*) are often now considered to be **recent additions** in the historical descriptions. In other words, many biblical scholars are now wondering whether these aspects of the textual stories may be not ancient reports about genocidal violence but rather these stories are edited reports and some of the details may well date to the time after the Exile (post–587 BCE). As horrific as it is to imagine it, these genocidal reports of killing all living things **may actually have been added to these battle reports in the years after the Exile**. This is not to say that some of them may have been older—after all, we do have reports of similar calls for violent bans in a Moabite inscription, for example, the Mesha Stele (dated to approx. 830 BCE).[21] But even here, the Moabite stone is a proclamation for public consumption, in many ways equivalent to public announcements that "The King is Very Angry." Ironically, this example of the ban was actually directed against the Israelites.

There have been ongoing debates and discussions about the historical role of the practice of genocidal violence, and we understand a great deal more about this than we did before (largely, perhaps, because many historians understandably found the whole subject a distasteful theme for study). But recent work suggests that we examine the use of these kinds of angry terms and violent language as *rhetoric*. When we read these descriptions of destruction of all living things—women and children included—are we really so far from descriptions like the following clearly post-exilic sentiment:

> **Psalm 137:8-9:** O daughter Babylon, you devastator! Happy shall they be who pay you back what you have done to us! Happy shall they be who take your little ones and dash them against the rock!

Recall that later post-exilic stories include punishment of the enemies of the Jews in equally genocidal language. In the telling of these otherwise charming tales, these details are gracefully left unmentioned in the presence of children, but they exist nonetheless. The end of the book of Esther includes the permission to kill the whole family of any who would threaten Israelites:

> **Esther 8:11:** By these letters the king allowed the Jews who were in every city to assemble and defend their lives, to destroy, to kill, and to annihilate any armed force of any people or province that might attack them, with their children and women, and to plunder their goods.

And in the next chapter, the even more chilling image:

> **Esther 9:5:** So the Jews struck down all their enemies with the sword, slaughtering, and destroying them, and did as they pleased to those who hated them.

In the book of Daniel, when those who plotted against Daniel and had him thrown to the lions are discovered, the punishment they intended for Daniel is handed out to the evil advisors of King Darius:

> **Daniel 6:24:** The king gave a command, and those who had accused Daniel were brought and thrown into the den of lions— they, their children, and their wives. Before they reached the bottom of the den the lions overpowered them and broke all their bones in pieces.

Once again, these violent themes are deeply troubling, but it is hard to avoid the observation that these violent images are the rhetoric of violence that is an essential aspect of tales deeply colored by anger and resentment. Further, they are written decades—even centuries—after an era when Israelites could have actually engaged in this kind of tactic on any battlefield. I believe that we **must** keep in mind that these expressions of violence come from a time when the Hebrew people were most certainly **not actually capable** of engaging in anything like this level of destructive violence against resented enemies. Once again, one is reminded of Frantz Fanon, who writes of the "colonized people's dreams," dreams of rising up and destroying the colonizer communities—these are angry fantasies and invariably quite graphic.[22] In sum, what I am suggesting is this: a good deal of the violent imagery of biblical narrative is a measure of anger and frustration. It is not necessarily a narrative of historical practices, and even less an instruction manual for terrorism, but it is a collective rage against the suffering of conquest and exile.

These historical realities behind the rhetoric prevent us from having too cheerful a view of the point of these stories—they are hardly appropriate (at least in their entirety) to children's Sunday school lessons—but they may be understandable in the context of anger.

Descriptions of the death of whole families is historically significant. Listen to the anguished voice of the book of Lamentations, describing the scene in Jerusalem after the fall of the city to the Babylonians:

> **Lamentations 2:21-22:** The young and the old are lying on the ground in the streets; my young women and my young men have fallen by the sword; in the day of your anger you have killed them, slaughtering without mercy. You invited my enemies from all around as if for a day of festival; and on the day of the anger of the LORD no one escaped or survived; those whom I bore and reared my enemy has destroyed.

They may well have been spoken by those who would actually wish to engage in such violence, but I believe that we must read these motifs of "kill them all!" in the context of the rhetoric of anger following the Exile. It is dangerous talk, but can we expect "nice" discussions in the heat of violence and injustice—or in the memories of devastation?

My point is this—reading descriptions of miraculous wars and devastation of enemies (and their entire families) is not the calm literature of real policy or serious intentions—it is the language of anguish and anger. Can we read these ventings of emotions—even the horrific imagery used—with historical appreciation of the realities of suffering that give rise to such emotion? And even more, can we , therefore, come to understand that there can be a poetics of violent language that can be associated with real violence or with no violence at all, particularly in circumstances where the rhetoric is used among marginalized, powerless, or defeated peoples?

LESSONS FOR COYOTES NO. 1: LEARN TO LISTEN TO ANGER

It would be a serious mistake to take biblical descriptions of miraculous wars and destruction and annihilation and proceed to literally draw maps and strategies with them—as if actual strategies can be gleaned from angry rhetoric. These biblical texts do not describe policy. It is an act of reckless irresponsibility to take angry rhetoric literally and excuse genocide. The fact that this is precisely what has happened in Christian history is, of course, all the more reason to insist that we read rhetoric as *rhetoric* and understand it for what it is. Furthermore, the practice of publishing Bible atlases that feature attempted drawings of biblical "war strategies" in various campaigns contributes to this militarization of biblical rhetoric. I would argue that the Bible's rhetoric should be a training book for learning to listen to angry pain. But why listen? Precisely because coyotes will often be in the position of confronting anger because they risk listening.

One of the most serious mistakes in modern, much less ancient, statecraft has been the fact that angry rhetoric has not been taken as a sign that further discussions should take place. Too often, angry rhetoric has been taken as a sign that discussions aren't possible. Precisely when they are most needed, negotiation is often rejected as a tactic. Yet, it seems only sane to think that in the face of threats, it is precisely negotiations that are critically needed. A political statement from a group that is filled with anger and resentment ought to bring forth an invitation to sit down and talk, not a shocked warning to fight anyone who would talk like that. In the face of world leaders who, for example, have called for studies of the holocaust because they insinuate that it did not happen, the response should not be threats of violence. Instead of threats, the response should be: make copies of the volumes of horrendous proof, buy copies of the many books and studies, send survivors and witnesses. In short: send in the historians, not the marines. This is the way of wisdom.

Part of my reason for thinking this way is the further realization that violent language often describes anger and suffering—it does not necessarily describe serious policy. When read as the language of anger, we can read such descriptions of war—including the wish for God to intervene and destroy our enemies for us when we cannot—as the psychology of grief and the rhetoric of anger. It need not be interpreted as expressions of policy or actual intentions to engage in genocide. What I am suggesting is that the language of violence in the Bible must be listened to for what it often really is—the language of anguish and anger, not advice for soldiers.

What does this do to a reading of Revelation? Virtually all modern scholars of Revelation agree that oppression and Roman violence against the Christian community play a role in the emotional language of Revelation—Rome is being threatened with God's punishment because of the suffering of the Christians in Palestine, even if perhaps the Christians were not as badly treated in Asia Minor. I would like to propose that we read Revelation with a sympathetic ear to the anger and suffering of the early Christians and not as some kind of contradictory policy statement that would dismiss the nonviolence of Jesus. Nobody is advocating physical warfare in Revelation. Like Paul at times, however, there is plenty of angry imagery and expressions of outrage and even, perhaps, some spiteful warnings about God's judgment of evil. Such language invites the nonviolent follower of Jesus to double his or her efforts at nonviolent action—not recoiling in shock that anyone would speak like this.

Paul, too, drew his militant imagery from Hebrew tradition. The book of Isaiah contains three rather significant motifs that will become important in later biblical thought. First is the transformation of the term "sword" to refer to the teachings of the Prophet: "He made my mouth like a sharp *sword*, in the shadow of his hand he hid me; he made me a polished arrow, in his quiver he hid me away" (Isa. 49:2). This is then developed elsewhere in Isaiah into a full-blown suit of spiritual armor:

> **Isaiah 59:17-18:** He put on righteousness like a breastplate, and a helmet of salvation on his head; he put on garments of vengeance for clothing, and wrapped himself in fury as in a mantle. According to their deeds, so will he repay; wrath to his adversaries, requital to his enemies; to the coastlands he will render requital.

These images are repeated and developed somewhat about one hundred years before the time of Jesus, in the book known as the Wisdom of Solomon (Wisdom 5:17-23). But Jesus and early Christianity will take up this imagery to quite different impact. Jesus will speak of a "sword" that separates the old "peace"— meaning old loyalties, even family loyalties. What is particularly fascinating is that this spiritual sword will even make former enemies into one's family members:

> **Matthew 10:34-36:** "Do not think that I have come to bring peace to the earth; I have not come to bring peace, but a sword. For I have come to set a man against his father, and a daughter against her mother, and a daughter-in-law against her mother-in-law; and one's foes will be members of one's own household."

Finally, the imagery of Revelation takes this one further step and portrays the victory of Christ over sin and violence to be a final battle. Included in this is the apparent imagery—borrowed clearly from Old Testament themes—of punishing "the nations":

Revelation 19:15: From his mouth comes a sharp sword with which to strike down the nations, and he will rule them with a rod of iron; he will tread the wine press of the fury of the wrath of God the Almighty.

This punishment of "the nations" can get quite graphic in John's rhetoric:

Revelation 19:17-18: Then I saw an angel standing in the sun, and with a loud voice he called to all the birds that fly in midheaven, "Come, gather for the great supper of God, to eat the flesh of kings, the flesh of captains, the flesh of the mighty, the flesh of horses and their riders—flesh of all, both free and slave, both small and great."

This death is accomplished by the sword from the mouth of the rider, clearly symbolizing Jesus:

Revelation 19:21: And the rest were killed by the sword of the rider on the horse, the sword that came from his mouth; and all the birds were gorged with their flesh.

But after the battle, quite miraculously, the nations are still alive, in order to appreciate their new life in the kingdom of God established by the great battle with sin and death:

Revelation 21:24-26: *The nations will walk by its light, and the kings of the earth will bring their glory into it.* Its gates will never be shut by day—and there will be no night there. People will bring into it the glory and the honor of the nations.

The writer of Revelation, even more so than Jesus and Paul, is capable of using even the most violent imagery of warfare, but without intending to describe, in the words of Paul, a battle "with flesh and blood." But it is warfare just the same—the kind of spiritual warfare that expects results in the real world of injustice, sin, confusion, suffering, and death. It is, in other words, an expression of the "Lamb's War"—but with the expectation that this Lamb's War has actual implications for how life is to be lived as the people of God in this world. It is real work—people might get upset.

I would humbly plead that we not only read the Bible with an ear for the cries of anguished anger from the suffering but also use this skill to listen to the anguished anger of present "enemies." It is precisely the angry words of modern political rhetoric that unfortunately convince some Western Christians that anyone who speaks with angry images and destructive language cannot possibly be reasoned with, or cannot be negotiated with. But if we are honest, then we know that anger is in all of us. The ability to listen beyond the anger, stay seated, and continue to seek terms of coexistence is the gift often developed by those who seek to cross borders in the name of peace. Learning to listen to pain is a deeply biblical lesson because there is a great deal of angry pain expressed in its pages. Sometimes we can turn violent biblical images into the rhetoric of change ("spiritual warfare," etc.), but this is always a tactic that is fraught with difficulty because it risks being misunderstood as a defense of violence.

Being able to live nonviolently, listen to violence, and continue to act for change in the face of anger, is the call of a Christian activist. It is the living embodiment of Jesus' instruction to be as peaceful as doves, but as clever as serpents. It is the way of the good coyote.

Unfinished Conversations (While Scaling This World's Fences . . .)

The kinds of action that I hope will be inspired by this book are rather simple and straightforward: meetings, discussions, and changed minds. I believe that modern peacemaking begins with risking borders and crossing them. Virtually every community where Christians live has communities of "the other" not far away. It is time to cross borders and meet the others. It is time for white Christians to meet African, Asian, Native, and Hispanic Americans. It is time for French Christians to meet Algerian-French immigrants. It is time for German and Scandinavian Christians to meet the Turkish and Syrian guest-worker communities and immigrants who are now part of their society but often still are an unknown people. For some of us in North America, it is time to violate American foreign policies of separation and hatred and go to Mexico, to Iran, to Russia—and listen. Whenever we are told to hate, we have just received our marching orders—to cross the borders that hate builds. Whenever we are told to preserve borders against "them," it is time for biblical coyotes to pack their bags, cross the borders, and start discussions.

A CONFESSION

I have come to believe that the early twenty-first century is not a very promising time for preaching the gospel. When I was growing up in the 1960s and 1970s, I would never have believed that the name of Jesus would ever become so abused and denigrated and used in the same breath with attitudes of hate, power, and greed. But it has happened—it is a time when Christians of good will are often forced to disavow the words and actions of many people who use the name of Jesus. Perhaps, just perhaps, it is also a time when followers of Jesus the Good Coyote should speak less—and act more.

There may come a day when the name of Jesus is not so deeply associated with terribly cruel behavior and attitudes, but it is not today. I am, quite frankly, deeply ashamed of the statements of many who speak the name of Jesus to justify their actions. I believe that it is now a time when non-Christians around the world will no longer be convinced of the love of Jesus by the volume or intensity of our shouts, the number of our leaflets or bumper stickers, or the political strategies to keep "the right people" in office. I believe that it is a time when non-Christians will only be impressed by Jesus embodied in our lives and actions, and some may not only be impressed but actually astounded—so jaundiced a view have they developed because of the incessant chatter of the "Christian Right" in North America.

I am not so confident that I have myself figured out the many ways we must work to restore the integrity of the confession of Christian faith, nor am I confident that I have not myself contributed to problems rather than solutions. I do, however, believe that the way forward will involve crossing borders, and that this will involve developing some skills.

LESSONS FOR COYOTES: PREPARING FOR DANGERS IN CROSSING BORDERS

In work for peace and justice, we always take risks. If our Christian peace work involves becoming a border crosser, then be forewarned—you will face a number of potentially abusive situations from your own "side" of the border. After you "cross," you will also find people who may give you a cool—or even hostile—reception on the "other side." It is best to think about some of these situations before you face them.

First of all, biblical coyotes and border crossers will be accused of being naive, so we need to be as informed as possible before crossing borders. Be ready for the accusation that "No one over there wants to talk ... they don't listen to reason...." But also be ready by reading and listening, and becoming alive to the issues that inform anger and resentment. We are crossing borders to listen first and foremost, but border crossers should be informed.

Second, border crossers will be accused of being traitors. Be ready for the accusation that you have betrayed "your people" because you are willing to accept criticism and consider the possibility that the "others" may have a legitimate complaint. Seek strength in your faith and seek strength in your fellow border crossers. But, don't be surprised with less-than-supportive attitudes if you cross borders.

Third, once you cross, border crossers will be accused of being spies. Are you really interested in learning about other people's viewpoints? Or, are you simply wanting to defend your side of the border? Are you ready to listen to anger and consider the possibility that they have legitimate reasons for anger? If you must listen to anger, be patient because many people around the world have every right to be angry. The only way to earn trust is to be willing to listen.

Fourth: border crossers will be accused of being "tourists." Are you prepared to do something with the information you gain? Are you simply wishing to meet with people in order to seek an exotic experience, or are you really working for change? Often it depends on how willing you are to return to your "side" with new information to offer others. If you are not willing to challenge prejudices and attitudes on your side of the "border," then you aren't really ready to violate borders.

Fifth: border crossers will be accused of being prisoners or refugees. Are you crossing because you have no choice? If so, then you can be easily dismissed as merely powerless. Another version of this is that you are accused of being a deviant. You are so unlike the others on your "side" (or in your group) that you are unable to have any influence. Think about this: we are often tempted to say in our own defense that "I am not like those others." But the further we distance ourselves from our own societies and backgrounds, the less useful we become as bridge people and border crossers. Perhaps you are a refugee with little ability to "return." If this is the case, then one might as well admit it up front. The accusation of being a deviant, however, can be one of the most devastating criticisms because it is often quite true—you come from a small group without great influence and you are not a major political figure or a leader. Have no fear, however, and trust in the power of taking first steps. Change must begin somewhere.

Finally, border crossers can be made into heroes. This is one of the most insidious problems of all because it is so gloriously tempting. If you are made into a hero, then you are also an unusual person from the other side and can be made into an impossible example precisely because you are so heroic. The founder of the Catholic Worker movement, a radical Catholic organization for social change, was Dorothy Day. When someone once called her a "saint," she replied, "You aren't going to write me off that easily!" The problem is that "heroes" become removed from the real world where the "regular people" live. If peace cannot be part of the real lives of the real people, but only the lives of the heroes, then it is easy to dismiss as impossible.

FIRST THOUGHTS ON COYOTE STRATEGIES: SMALL IS BEAUTIFUL

How, then, can we begin the steps of peacemaking and border crossing? At the end of most presentations that I have given, or presentations that I have heard about pressing social issues, invariably a well-meaning person will stand and ask, "So what can we **do**?" This is always an interesting question, but I have come to understand that it is also a minefield. First of all, not all theorists are also good strategists, so it can be tempting to venture into a discussion of subjects where one is not very proficient. I am mainly an educator, writer, and speaker, even if I have had ambitions at times to be more directly involved in issues and "do something." There is always a temptation for educators to forget that education that is truly empowering **is** "doing something," whether that education takes place in a classroom, editing a newspaper, or producing an online video production. It can be difficult to resist the sneering comment, "Those who can't do— teach!" but this is a false argument. Effective action always requires thought, planning, and a foundation, and Christian action always requires contemplation, prayer, and study.

I am interested in the reasons "why" and, therefore, the theological and biblical ideas that *inspire* action, but I need to defer to (and listen to) more experienced activists and strategists when it comes to the obvious question of "action." So, the first problem with the question, "What can I do?" is not the question, but the temptation to answer it without experience. When I make suggestions in this conclusion to our study, I am not making them as an "expert" in organizing, but as a participant, observer, and frankly, a dreamer.

The second problem is this: as soon as you suggest a particular action that someone takes issue with, some may actually believe that the issue is somehow "dismissed" or less important just because the particular suggested *action* is questioned or debated. This is an old debating trick, and it is a nasty one: question the example, or a detail, and then give the impression that the entire issue is questionable.

There is a variation on the second problem—also a very old debating tactic—still very popular despite its antiquity, and you will see it every week on television. This is the tactic of attacking the *presenter* rather than the issue. For example, speakers or presenters can be confronted with hostile questions like: "So, what are **you** doing about it?" Again, not everyone is a master strategist—we do what we can do. I believe that education is part of action. Strategy without preparation and thought is usually fruitless and wasted effort.

Finally, there is one last problem when dealing with the question, "What can we **do**?" In the modern, Hollywood-world, we often imagine ourselves engaged in action that is romantic, adventurous, and complete with the dynamic sound track in the background. When real projects seem less glamorous and have no sound track, we can make the mistake of believing that if our efforts are not the basis of a feature film, or at least a really good news story, they must not be "effective." I once heard Jim Wallis, the noted author and editor of *Sojourners Magazine*, refer years ago to "John Wayne Radical Christians." It was a wonderfully humorous image, and we all understood what he meant: there is a temptation to want to be "heroes" of the faith, not only to do "something" but also **look** like we are doing something big. The fact is, of course, that we all admire such "heroes" like Dr. King, Cesar Chavez, or Dorothy Day. But there is a problem here: succumbing to the false idea that if we don't start "Peace Ministries, Inc." or the "Peace Center," then we aren't successful and, therefore, we are not really "doing something." The thing is, even if we **do** start big projects, we can easily get bogged down in the day-to-day fund-raising to pay the bills of the "center" or the "office," and the original vision and enthusiasm flounders for lack of energy.

Big projects should start as small projects and small initiatives. Growth should come as it is needed, not growth for the sake of looking "big" and "impressive." "Heroic"-sized projects can be good, but their success (or lack of success) should not intimidate us into thinking that if our efforts aren't "big," then they are not valuable. Perhaps it's because I was raised in the tiny Christian movement of the Quakers and because my father raised his family running a corner drug store that I have come to understand the power of small projects and small business and small beginnings. Small, as E. F. Schumacher once taught us, is beautiful—and is usually very real in its impact on real people.

What I mean is simply this: if a church begins to "take action" for peace by simply inviting people to come together in the church basement and talk, don't be disappointed if crowds of people do not show up. Positive steps are positive steps. Just make coffee for thirty people and be happy if six interested people show up. Six is a start.

In my own work in higher education, for example, there is a temptation to think in terms of grandiose "projects" because they (1) attract positive attention (which is always assumed to be useful) and (2) may attract funding from foundations or businesses. This, however, has a down side—it means that small projects may seem insignificant or minor and, therefore, never even get started because a small organizing group (even an individual) gets discouraged. It is also dangerous because the people who operate foundations have an agenda, and they know very well that they can "bend" projects to accomplish their agendas because they have money to pass out. Sometimes, however, what needs to be done is not on the agenda of a wealthy foundation. The fact is that we need thousands of small efforts. Your effort may grow, or it may remain a valuable small contribution to the bigger picture.

SECOND THOUGHTS ON COYOTE STRATEGIES

Let me be as encouraging as I can and offer what strategic advice I can based on my own observations. The challenges facing any move toward Christian peacemaking actions in the twenty-first century include, in my view, creative planning so that they are biblically inspired actions that are characterized as: (1) Invitational, (2) Creative, (3) Entrepreneurial, (4) Hybrid, and (5) Digital. Let me explain each point.

I believe that any actions that are planned, either as a result of reading this work or many other important works on Christian peacemaking, ought to be **invitational**. That is, actions should, by their nature, be inviting to others so that they understand and can even participate. Our use of religious symbols, stories, and rituals ought to be as transparently positive and peaceful as possible. But, at the same time, we need not cave in to modern anti-religious sentiments that would suggest that we abandon all use of our symbols, stories, or rituals as "inappropriate." The symbols, stories, and rituals that we choose to feature in our projects, however, ought to be typified by their *inclusive, invitational, and open character* rather than being characterized by exclusion or appear to be the actions of only the devoted (and thus imply proselytizing masked as peacemaking). As Christian peacemakers, we should offer those gifts from within our various Christian traditions that invite participation in the common goals of peacemaking. So, begin by considering your potential audience and what would be the most positive and invitational use of symbols and phrases. Perhaps a group from within a denominational tradition (Lutheran? Methodist? Adventist?) ought to spend a bit of time studying their own tradition for the names of teachers, writers, or activists whose legacy or memory can be revived or honored with peacemaking action. If you are a participant in a Christian group that intentionally sustains a unique cultural identity, then search for the voices of peace and the peacemaking stories and traditions from within your cultural tradition. What I believe we should anticipate by our names and symbolism is the easy accusation made by opponents who would suggest that peacemaking is somehow a "foreign" idea that is not a part of our traditions.

Second, our actions should be **creative** and make use of the gifts of many people within our tradition—gifts of art and music and story as well as careful and critical religious analysis and thought. Performance, for example, offered as a gift is by its very nature invitational. But it can also help to "cross borders." Perhaps we should be willing to encourage not only the performance and creative arts from within "our" various traditions—religious and cultural—but also radically cross the borders and feature the performance arts of the people whom we are told are our "enemies." Highlighting the performance arts (poetry? paintings? carvings? songs? plays?) of those peoples or nations we are told are our "enemies" can sometimes be a highly effective means of challenging the borders that leaders try to draw between us. It is hard to say "those people" when we read their poetry, listen to their songs, or admire their painting. It is also not threatening and may serve to open minds to consider other important ideas.

Third, the reality of modern action is that it must often find ways to finance itself creatively and with some innovation. This is what I mean by peacemaking that is **entrepreneurial**. How can we harness the ever-present reality of consumption toward the ends of peacemaking? The "Fair Trade" movement, in which producers in developing countries are offered fair and just wages for their production as opposed to oppressive and minimal-level compensation from the dictates of corporate greed, is a wonderful start. How can our peacemaking and advocacy of nonviolence translate into the consumption of "the products of peace" and, thus, also generate the funds necessary for the work to continue? Honest, consistent, and effective fund-raising for sustaining projects should be part of the first discussions.

It is one thing to participate in boycotts of products from companies who practice unethical business practices, but it is even more creative to encourage the consumption of products from those companies that go out of their way to run ethical businesses and pay the workers a decent wage.

Whatever political system we ultimately advocate, consumption is a human reality, and we can no longer afford (literally) to associate peacemaking with lack of creative and financial wisdom. This is an invitation to set free the work of peace, rather than chain it to the whims of corporate foundations or trusts, or the political winds of change. In other words, we must also be about the "business" of peace. I am inspired by my Quaker predecessors whose business success transformed the ability of the Quaker movement to function. These are models that ought to be examined anew. We need the gifted entrepreneurs to help fuel the furnaces of social change.

Fourth, peacemaking in the modern world must be **"hybrid"**— expressed in terms that communicate the cross-cultural, multicultural, and transcultural realities of the modern world. To draw on our various traditions is not the same thing as being chained to traditional means or methods of expressing those traditions. Furthermore, we can borrow from one another as an expression of solidarity with one another. This is both an opportunity but also a danger. We must never "appropriate" a tradition from outside our own faith tradition without the full participation of those from whom this tradition is borrowed. Let us no longer, for example, borrow drums or rituals from Native American spirituality without Native permission or participation in their use. We must no longer use symbols or rituals with little care for their context and traditional meanings for the groups from whom they are drawn. Being a border crosser means learning to be open and respectful of the differences between peoples and using those differences as a way to coexist and learn from one another. Just the act of asking permission can build wonderful bridges, whether the answer is yes or no.

Finally, I would suggest that our work must be **"digital."** By this I merely invite us all to make full use of the potentially dramatic impact of communication technologies from the Internet to the use of simple video and audio devices to spread a message of peace against the sophisticated use of these technologies by the purveyors of hatred. There is much to be learned here. Progressive-minded Christians in previous decades of the twentieth century foolishly ignored or abandoned many forms of media to fundamentalist ranters. Early radio and then television opportunities were often left to hucksters and demagogues who used these powerful media tools to spread messages of anger and hatred. This was a strategic mistake of major proportions. All of these practical thoughts require cooperation and mutual instruction since few of us master all of these skills and ideas. But this is precisely the point—peacemaking is by definition a communal act, and we all contribute toward the success.

There are easy places to begin, but one of the best is to assemble a study group that wishes to read together to bring thoughts and hopes together. I hope that this book can be a useful reading project that inspires action, but there also are many others that are wonderful resources for thinking together about these issues. For Christians, I strongly recommend a Bible study to begin, moving toward the more practical guides for action, mainly because I believe that a strong foundation in the ethical and spiritual roots of peacemaking will continue to guide action. Action without contemplation, prayer, and discussion can be a horrendous exercise in frustration and futility.

As the group gains strength (and this may mean inward strength more than numbers of people) then action needs to begin by informing each other of the details of the issues that you decide to focus on. Inform yourself. Invite speakers and resource people to share their experience and observations. As a Quaker, I believe in the notion that as we pray and discuss, we open ourselves to the movement of the Spirit of God among us, and ideas will emerge, some of which may begin to build a unified vision. Don't try to "do everything." Seek a focus and short-term goals that will contribute to the unified vision. If more than one focus persists, deal with one and then the other, and then evaluate which of the ideas seems to energize people the most. Some ideas are not bad, but are simply not for the time and need to be put off for another time. Above all, keep a sense of humor and a sense of support for each other because it is precisely in walking together in love and support that we begin to become aware that another is walking with us on our roads across the borders, which are often the same roads that lead to Emmaus.

Notes

Introduction

1. Samuel Huntington, *The Clash of Civilizations and the Remaking of World Order* (New York: Simon and Schuster, 1998).

2.. For an important reply to the "Clash of Civilizations" theory, see *The New Crusades: Constructing the Muslim Enemy,* ed. Emran Qureshi and Michael A. Sells (New York: Columbia University Press, 2003), most particularly the essays by the late Edward Said, "The Clash of Definitions," 68-87; John Trumpbour, "The Clash of Civilizations: Samuel P. Huntington, Bernard Lewis, and the Remaking of the Post-Cold War World Order," 88-130; and Roy Mottahedeh, "The Clash of Civilizations: An Islamist's Critique," 131-51.

3. I have benefited immensely from the insights of three works in particular on these issues: *In God's Name: Genocide and Religion in the Twentieth Century,* ed. Omer Bartov and Phyllis Mack (New York, Oxford: Berghahn Books, 2001); *Studies in Comparative Genocide,* ed. Levon Chorbajian and George Shirinian (Great Britain: Macmillan, 1999); and for a fascinating series of historical essays, *The Massacre in History,* ed. Mark Levene and Penny Roberts (New York, Oxford: Berghahn Books, 1999).

4. See *Propaganda and Persuasion,* ed. Garth Jowett and Victoria O'Donnell (London, New Delhi: Sage Publications, 2005).

5. Readers interested in knowing more about some of these "coyotes" can find the following: Taner Akçam, *From Empire to Republic: Turkish Nationalism and the Armenian Genocide* (London: Zed Books, 2004). Ronald G. Suny normally specializes in Soviet and Georgian history and politics, but see also his Armenian history, *Looking Toward Ararat: Armenia in Modern History* (Bloomington: Indiana University, 1993). On Uri Avnery, see *My Friend, the Enemy* (Westport: L. Hill, 1986). On Mahmoud Taha, the "African Gandhi," see *The Second Message of Islam* (Syracuse: Syracuse University Press, 1996). On historic opposition to crusades, see Palmer Throop, *Criticism of the Crusade: A Study of Public Opinion and Crusade Propaganda* (London: Porcupine Press, 1975), and Benjamin Kedar, *Crusade and Mission* (Princeton: Princeton University Press, 1984). On modern

border violators, see Renny Golden and Michael McConnell, *Sanctuary: The New Underground Railroad* (New York: Orbis Books, 1986). On John Woolman, see *The Journal of John Woolman and A Plea for the Poor* (New York: Citadel Press, 1972).

Chapter One: Hearing Silenced Voices of the Bible

1. See, for example, Calum Carmichael, *The Origins of the Biblical Law: The Decalogues and the Book of the Covenant* (New York: Cornell University Press, 1992); James Watts, *Reading Law: The Rhetorical Shaping of the Pentateuch* (Sheffield: Sheffield Academic Press, 1999); Cyril Rodd, *Glimpses of a Strange Land: Studies in Old Testament Ethics* (Edinburgh: T&T Clark, 2001); and William Johnstone, "The 'Ten Commandments': Some Recent Interpretations," in *The Expository Times* 100:453-59.

2. David J. A. Clines, *Interested Parties: The Ideology of Writers and Readers of the Hebrew Bible*, JSOT Suppl. 205 (Sheffield: JSOT Press, 1995), 33.

Chapter Two: Violent Times and Courageous Hopes

1. I have gone into much greater detail on my analysis of the Babylonian Exile in my work *A Biblical Theology of Exile* (Minneapolis: Fortress Press, 2002) and the older work, *The Religion of the Landless: A Sociology of the Babylonian Exile* (Bloomington: Meyer-Stone, 1989). But see also Rainer Albertz, *Israel in Exile: The History and Literature of the Sixth Century B.C.E.* (Atlanta: The Society of Biblical Literature, 2003) and Oded Lipshits and Joseph Blenkinsopp, eds., *Judah and the Judeans in the Neo-Babylonian Period* (Winona Lake: Eisenbrauns, 2003).

2. See Paul Bentley Kern, *Ancient Siege Warfare* (Bloomington: Indiana University Press, 1999).

3. See the helpful summary by Bill Arnold, *Who Were the Babylonians?* (Atlanta: Society for Biblical Literature, 2004).

4. *Ancient Near Eastern Texts*, ed. J. Pritchard (Princeton: Princeton University Press, 1950), Document 564—thus March 15/16, 597?

5. See page 218, in Oded Lipshits, *The Fall and Rise of Jerusalem* (Winona Lake: Eisenbrauns, 2005).

6. Lipshits, 270.

7. Lawrence Stager, "The Fury of Babylon: Ashkelon and the Archaeology of Destruction," *Biblical Archaeology Review* 22:1 (1996): 96.

8. See especially Klaus Wengst, *Pax Romana and the Peace of Jesus Christ* (Minneapolis: Fortress Press, 1987), and more recently the important work of Richard Horsley, *Jesus and Empire: The Kingdom of God and the New World Disorder* (Minneapolis: Fortress Press, 2002).

9. Wengst, 13.

10. Wengst, 52-53.

11. Bruce Malina, *The Social World of Jesus and the Gospels* (New York and London: Routledge, 1996). See also his *The Social Gospel of Jesus: The Kingdom of God in Mediterranean Perspective* (Minneapolis: Fortress, 2001), 45.

12. Wengst, 28.

13. Marcus J. Borg, *Conflict, Holiness, and Politics in the Teachings of Jesus* (Harrisburg: Trinity Press International, 1998), 48.

14. Borg, 49.

15. Wengst, 30.

16. Horsley, 13.

17. Wengst, 27.

18. See Steven J. Friesen, *Imperial Cults and the Apocalypse of John: Reading Revelation in the Ruins* (Oxford: Oxford University Press, 2006 [new edition]); and Wes Howard-Brook and Anthony Gwyther, *Unveiling Empire: Reading Revelation Then and Now* (Maryknoll: Orbis Books, 1999).

19. Richard Horsley, *Jesus and the Spiral of Violence* (Minneapolis: Fortress Press, 1992). This discussion was taken up again by Richard Horsley and Walter Wink in *The Love of Enemy and Nonretaliation in the New Testament*, ed. Willard Swartley (Philadelphia: Westminster/John Knox Press, 1992).

20. Jacob Neusner, *A Life of Rabban Yohanan ben Zakkai* (Leiden: Brill, 1962), 20. See also Neusner, *Development of a Legend: Studies in the Traditions Concerning Yohanan ben Zakkai* (Leiden: E. J. Brill, 1970).

21. Jacob Z. Lauterbach, *Mekilta de-Rabbi Ishmael: A Critical Edition on the Basis of the Manuscripts and Early Editions with an English Translation, Introduction, and Notes* (Philadelphia: Jewish Publication Society, 1933/1961).

22. Louis Finkelstein, *The Pharisees: The Sociological Background of Their Faith*, vol. 1 and 2 (Philadelphia: The Jewish Publication Society of America: 1938 [1962]), 286-91.

23. Salo W. Baron, *A Social and Religious History of the Jews*, vol. 11, *The Christian Era* (New York: Columbia University Press, 1937 [1967, new and revised edition]), 114-15.

24. Neusner, *A Life*, 142.

25. A good introduction to progressive participants in this debate rarely heard in American news sources would be Roane Carey and Jonathan Shainin, eds., *The Other Israel: Voices of Refusal and Dissent* (New York: The New Press, 2002), as well as materials available from The Jewish Peace Fellowship: http://www.jewish-peacefellowship.org/

Chapter Three: "Second Isaiah and Jonah"

1. See Vine Deloria, "Out of Chaos," *Parabola* 10:1 (1985).

Chapter Four: Crossing Over for Peace

1. I have relied heavily on Bruce Routledge's very helpful book on Moabite history and archaeology, *Moab in the Iron Age: Hegemony, Polity, Archaeology* (Philadelphia: University of Pennsylvania Press, 2004). For the Mesha Inscription, see Routledge's discussion in 133-53, and also Simon B. Parker, *Stories in Scripture and Inscriptions: Comparative Studies on Narratives in Northwest Semitic Inscriptions and the Hebrew Bible* (New York: Oxford University Press, 1997).

2. See translations by Sandra Landis Gogel in *A Grammar of Epigraphic Hebrew* (Atlanta: Scholars Press, 1998), 393-95.

3. Routledge states: "I would argue that conceptually, the key to invoking herem is the prevention of exchange through the insertion of the deity, who holds booty and captives as inalienable (nonexchangeable) possessions. In preventing exchange, one prevents the formation of a mutually recognized relationship," 150.

4. It may be significant that this note about Edom's revolt immediately follows the condemnation of Jehoram for "doing evil in the sight of the Lord"—the standard Deuteronomic dismissal of royalty.

5. Lawrence Turner, *Genesis* (Sheffield: Sheffield Academic Press, 2000), 115.

6. R. Christopher Heard, *Dynamics of Diselection: Ambiguity in Genesis 12–36 and Ethnic Boundaries in Post-Exilic Judah,* Semeia Studies 39, (SBL: Atlanta, 2001), 106-7.

7. William McKane, *Studies in the Patriarchal Narratives* (Edinburgh: Handsell Press, 1979), 128.

8. Turner, 109.

9. Gerhard Von Rad, *Genesis* (London: SCM, 1961), 261.

10. Seth D. Kunin, *The Logic of Incest: A Structuralist Analysis of Hebrew Mythology,* JSOT Supplement Series no. 185 (Sheffield: Sheffield Academic Press, 1995), 114.

11. See Claus Westermann's discussion in *Genesis 1-11: A Commentary* (Minneapolis: Augsburg Press, 1984), especially his fascinating Introduction.

12. I develop the tradition of penitential prayer as a post-exilic form in some detail in my work *A Biblical Theology of Exile* (Minneapolis: Fortress Press, 2002).

Chapter Five: The New Creationism

1. I would like to especially thank Reverend Scott and Susan Stork-Finley of Melbourne, Australia, for their influence and suggestions along these lines.

2. Richard Clifford, *Creation in the Biblical Accounts,* ed. Richard J. Clifford and John J. Collins, *Catholic Biblical Quarterly* Monograph Series 24 (Washington, D.C.: Catholic Biblical Assn. of America, 1992), 7. See also Richard J. Clifford, "The Roots of Apocalypticism in Near Eastern Myth," *The Encyclopedia of Apocalypticism,* ed. John J. Collins, vol. 1—The Origins of Apocalypticism in Judaism and Christianity (New York: Continuum, 1998), 3-38.

3. After writing the initial draft of this chapter, I was delighted to discover the work of J. Richard Middleton, *The Liberating Image: The Imago Dei in Genesis 1* (Grand Rapids: Brazos Press, 2005), who articulates ideas similar to those presented in this part of the chapter, especially in his chapter six, "Created in the Image of a Violent God?" Middleton's analysis of Genesis 1, however, is quite a bit fuller than my attempts here, and I am pleased to recommend it for those who wish to pursue this line of thinking on Genesis further.

4. Clifford, 7.

5. Mark Smith, "The Baal Cycle" (81-180), in *Ugaritic Narrative Poetry,* ed. Simon B. Parker, vol. 9—Society of Biblical Literature: Writings from the Ancient World (Atlanta: Scholars Press, 1997), 85.

6. Claus Westermann, *Genesis 37–50,* trans. John Scullion, SJ (Philadelphia: Augsburg, 1984).

7. My thinking about the nonviolence of the book of Daniel was originally inspired by my study of the works of John J. Collins, whose writings on the book of Daniel represent some of the most important writing in the twentieth century on this fascinating book. See J. J. Collins, *The Apocalyptic Visions of the Book of Daniel* (Missoula: Scholars Press, 1977), as the earlier statement and his *Daniel, A Commentary,* in the Hermeneia Series (Minneapolis: Fortress Press, 1993) for a very sophisticated and thorough treatment of issues related to Daniel. My own work on "The Book of Daniel" is in vol. 7 of *The New Interpreter's Bible* (Nashville: Abingdon Press, 1996), 17-194.

8. Crawford Toy, *Proverbs* (Edinburgh: T&T Clark, 1999), 333. Toy compares this with the Greek virtue of *sophrosyne,* but notably, North's impressively sweeping survey of this virtue in Greek literature includes no examples of this virtue as a con-